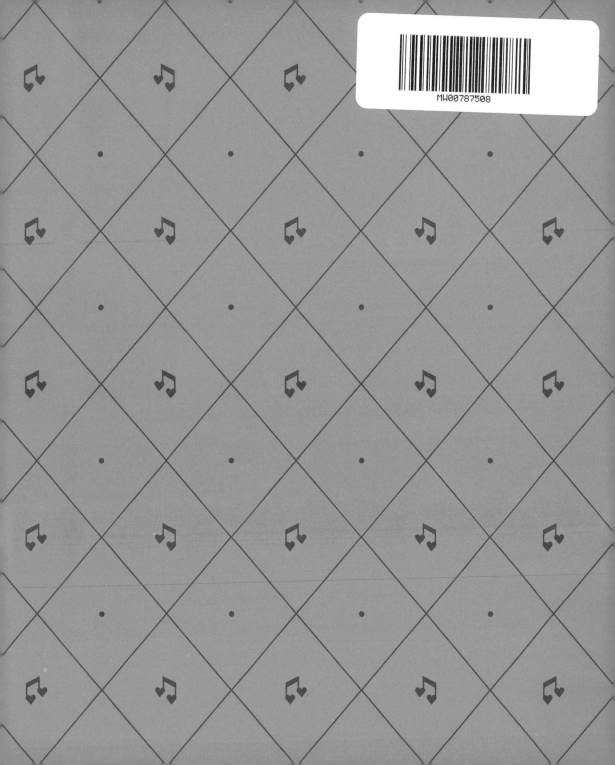

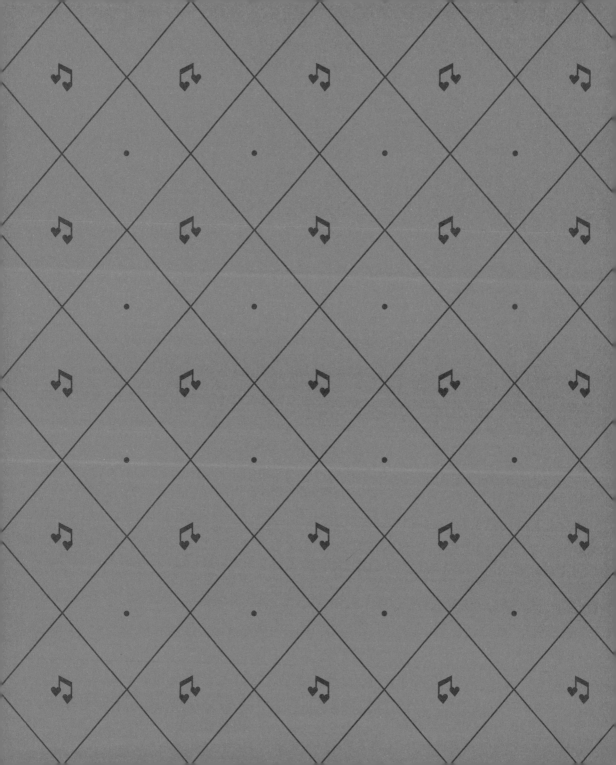

WE FOUND
LOVE,
Song by Song

WE FOUND LOVE,

Song by Song

The Stories Behind 100 Romantic Hits

ANNIE ZALESKI

Illustrated by Darling Clementine

RUNNING PRESS

PHILADELPHIA

Running Press
Hachette Book Group
1290 Avenue of the Americas, New York, NY 10104
www.runningpress.com
@Running_Press

First Edition: December 2024

Published by Running Press, an imprint of Hachette Book Group, Inc.
The Running Press name and logo are trademarks of Hachette Book Group, Inc.

The Hachette Speakers Bureau provides a wide range of authors for speaking events. To find
out more, go to www.hachettespeakersbureau.com or email HachetteSpeakers@hbgusa.com.

Running Press books may be purchased in bulk for business, educational, or promotional use. For more information, please
contact your local bookseller or the Hachette Book Group Special Markets Department at Special.Markets@hbgusa.com.

The publisher is not responsible for websites (or their content) that are not owned by the publisher.

Print book cover and interior design by Katie Benezra

Library of Congress Cataloging-in-Publication Data
Names: Zaleski, Annie, author. | Darling Clementine, illustrator.
Title: We found love, song by song : the stories behind 100 romantic hits / Annie Zaleski ; illustrated by Darling Clementine.
Description: First edition. | Philadelphia : Running Press, 2024. | Includes bibliographical references and index.
Summary: "Celebrate 100 of the most beloved love songs of all time with this beautiful hardcover keepsake that will make
    the perfect gift for loved ones at Valentine's Day or any time of year. Award-winning author and music journalist Annie
    Zaleski's collection offers readers fascinating history and behind-the-scenes stories about each love song's everlasting
    impact" —Provided by publisher.
Identifiers: LCCN 2023053373 (print) | LCCN 2023053374 (ebook) | ISBN 9780762487004 (hardcover) |
    ISBN 9780762487011 (ebook)
Subjects: LCSH: Love songs—History and criticism. | Popular music—United States—20th century—History and criticism. |
    Popular music—United States—21st century—History and criticism.
Classification: LCC ML3470 .Z35 2024 (print) | LCC ML3470 (ebook) | DDC 782.42164—dc23/eng/20231212
LC record available at https://lccn.loc.gov/2023053373
LC ebook record available at https://lccn.loc.gov/2023053374

ISBNs: 978-0-7624-8700-4 (hardcover), 978-0-7624-8701-1 (ebook)

Printed in China

APS

10 9 8 7 6 5 4 3 2 1

To my husband, Matt, a loving curator
of mix CDs full of love songs

CONTENTS

Introduction

LOVE SONGS HAVE existed almost as long as the emotion of love itself. Experts generally consider the poem "The Love Song for Shu-Sin," written in approximately 2000 BCE, as ground zero for the art form. Of course, love songs have evolved quite a bit since then, although their underlying sentiments remain remarkably similar: These songs capture the indescribable, intangible feeling when your heart overflows with affection and tenderness for someone else.

There are said to be more than 100 million love songs in existence today, a mind-blowing fact underscored by a 2018 study published in *Psychology of Music*: Between 1960 and 2010, 67.3 percent of top 40 songs mentioned love or relationships in their lyrics. This statistic begs the question: Why are there so many songs about love?

Love is universal to the human experience. We all want it—and we all crave it—but it's not always easy to find. And once you do find it? Good luck not letting it get away! But love songs bring us joy and remind us of happy moments from our lives when we did (and do) feel accepted and attractive. In times when we feel lonely, these songs remind us of what love feels like and that we're all capable of being loved. In other words, love songs ignite powerful feelings within us and offer hope for the future.

Songwriters often draw from their own lives when penning love songs, incorporating their own romantic experiences and relationships to create evocative and relatable music and lyrics—everything from love at first sight (INXS, "Never Tear Us Apart") and a first kiss (the Drifters, "This Magic Moment") to that butterflies-in-your-stomach crush (Guns N' Roses, "Sweet Child O' Mine"). Or dancing cheek to cheek (Paul Anka's "Put Your Head on My Shoulder"). Or loving someone so much you'd do *anything* for them (Marvin Gaye and Tammi Terrell, "Ain't No Mountain High Enough"). Or a fairy-tale romance you never want to end (Taylor Swift, "Love Story").

Of course, love songs aren't always upbeat. Some chronicle the soul-crushing, all-consuming, and totally exhausting experience of unrequited love, or the experience of yearning for the type of love you desire. Somewhat paradoxically, discussing romance through the lens of heartbreak or disappointment—for example, an overwhelming feeling of regret, as in Patsy Cline's "I Fall to Pieces"—can sometimes amplify the power of love. Lost love or not having your love reciprocated makes those successful relationships that much sweeter.

Many songs considered love songs aren't love songs at all—looking at you, Simple Minds' "Don't You (Forget About Me)"—but are actually about friendship. It makes sense, since most would agree that the best relationships tend to start with friendship as a foundation anyway.

On the cheekier side of things, some love songs aren't even about love for humans. The Beatles' "Martha My Dear" is a tender tune about Paul McCartney's beloved sheepdog. But having unorthodox origins doesn't make a love song any less valid or sentimental—after all, love itself takes on many forms.

Remember that you don't have to be happily partnered to enjoy and appreciate love songs either. Listening to them and reading about them offers an aspirational experience—the feeling that one day maybe you can find a loving companion and a wonderful relationship that's right for you.

In other words, love songs are for *everybody*—and so is this book. That's why these songs are arranged in chronological order by release year. Just as you can't judge the inherent value of a relationship, you can't rank the quality or impact of love songs. Choosing just 100 love songs is an impossible task, but that's exactly what this collection aims to do—capture the many dimensions of what it means to love and be loved. So grab your honey, cuddle up under a blanket, and settle in to learn the backstories about some of music's greatest love songs of all time.

THE WAY YOU LOOK TONIGHT

1936 · FRED ASTAIRE

Songwriters: Jerome Kern (music); Dorothy Fields (lyrics)

IN THE 1936 movie *Swing Time*, Fred Astaire takes to the piano and starts to play a lovely ballad called "The Way You Look Tonight." Ginger Rogers, who's washing her hair in the sink of an adjacent bathroom, overhears the performance and slowly walks into the room toward him. She gently touches Astaire on the shoulder, and the couple exchange a loving gaze as the song glides to an end.

Sounds impossibly romantic, right? Well, according to Hollywood gossip columnist Sidney Skolsky, the movie initially envisioned this moment as a comedic scene. Rogers's soapy, shampoo-covered head was to be played for laughs, as Astaire was "to tell [her] that she should always look as lovely as she did then." Luckily, director George Stevens recut the scene to instead emphasize the onscreen chemistry between the duo—a smart move, as "The Way You Look Tonight" is one of the most heartfelt love songs ever written.

The narrator tells his beloved that during darker times, he knows the mere thought of her beauty will sustain him. It's not just her comely smile and cheeks, either, but her little features—like the cute way her nose looks when she laughs— that provide solace. How she looks on this particular night is perfect and deserves to be preserved forever.

Of course, Astaire and Rogers weren't the only dynamic duo working on *Swing Time*. The composer-lyricist dream team of Jerome Kern and Dorothy Fields wrote some of the film's most memorable songs, including "The Way You Look Tonight." Kern was a prolific and celebrated musical composer responsible for songs like "Ol'

Man River" and "Smoke Gets in Your Eyes." Fields was equally respected, having penned the lyrics to indelible tunes such as "On the Sunny Side of the Street" and "I'm in the Mood for Love."

Together, the pair had recently collaborated on music for two 1935 films, *I Dream Too Much* and *Roberta*, so they were in a good groove as they approached *Swing Time*. "I always found Jerry easy to work with," Fields said in the book *They're Playing Our Song: Conversations with America's Classic Songwriters*. She was particularly affected by the part he came up with for "The Way You Look Tonight," adding, "The first time Jerry played that melody for me I went out and started to cry. The release absolutely killed me. I couldn't stop, it was so beautiful."

"The Way You Look Tonight" became a massive hit in the fall of 1936, reaching No. 1 on *Billboard*'s chart of best-selling sheet music. Versions of the song cut by Astaire, Guy Lombardo, and Teddy Wilson—the latter featuring vocals by Billie Holiday—all appeared on *Billboard* lists of popular records, and the song won the third-ever Academy Award for best song. Astaire's take understandably was particularly sentimental: Classy, debonair piano from Johnny Green mingles with low-lit orchestral accompaniment.

Over the years, "The Way You Look Tonight" has remained popular: Frank Sinatra made the song his own in a snappy 1964 cover; vocal group the Lettermen had their first hit with a cover, reaching No. 13 on the *Billboard* Hot 100 in 1961; and Tony Bennett cut the song as a duet with both country star Faith Hill and Mexican superstar Thalía.

UNFORGETTABLE

1951 · NAT KING COLE

Songwriter: Irving Gordon

CALLING SOMEONE "UNFORGETTABLE" is a supreme compliment—just about the highest compliment one can give. That goes double when it's a legend like Nat King Cole dishing out this flattering remark. On the 1951 romantic classic "Unforgettable," the title track of his 1952 LP, Cole gives one of his most memorable vocal performances—one that's sophisticated, soulful, generous, and deeply moving.

In fact, he's the perfect interpreter of a song centered on someone who's overcome with emotion while gazing upon a beautiful partner. The song's twist, however, is humility: The narrator of "Unforgettable" isn't just smitten—they're also grateful their love is reciprocated.

The tenderhearted song was written by Irving Gordon, a Brooklyn-born songwriter who wrote Billie Holiday's "Me, Myself and I," as well as songs cut by Perry Como and Patti Page. Cole recorded his take on August 17, 1951, with an orchestra conducted by Nelson Riddle. Between the elegant strings and Cole's performance, "Unforgettable" was popular on the radio *and* in stores, as the tune graced the top 30 of *Billboard*'s Best-Selling Pop Singles and Most Played by Jockeys charts.

Sadly, Cole died in 1965 of lung cancer; he was just 45 years old. Decades later, Cole's daughter, the soul/R&B star Natalie Cole, honored her father by covering songs he also recorded. The subsequent album, 1991's

Unforgettable . . . with Love, also featured her singing alongside him on a new version of "Unforgettable." Engineer Al Schmitt told *Sound on Sound* that the duet had emotional precedent. "When Natalie performed in Vegas, she would sing along to a video of Nat singing 'Unforgettable'—that's where the idea came from."

Fortuitously, Nat King Cole's original vocal take was captured on its own track, so the modern studio crew had an easier time merging the voices of father and daughter. With modern production polish, his voice sounds even richer and more sentimental, particularly when paired with Natalie's performance. She embraces the loving spirit of the song, but nostalgia suffuses her delivery; it's impossible not to interpret this new "Unforgettable" as also a love letter to her late father.

That take was an adult contemporary radio hit and reached No. 14 on the *Billboard* Hot 100, milestones that presaged an even bigger honor: winning three Grammy Awards, including the prestigious Song of the Year and Record of the Year trophies. The song has remained, well, unforgettable in history—after all, Cole's original 1951 recording was also inducted into the Grammy Hall of Fame in 2000.

LET'S DO IT (LET'S FALL IN LOVE)

1956 • ELLA FITZGERALD

Songwriter: Cole Porter

ANIMALS ARE POWERLESS to resist the lure of love. And that applies to *all* animals—not just humans, but also oysters, clams, goldfish, and even sponges. That's the playful underlying premise of the Cole Porter–penned "Let's Do It (Let's

Fall in Love)," which runs down all the living things that find themselves googly-eyed over a mate.

The song boasts winking lyrics that are double entendres—the titular "do it" possesses multiple meanings depending on perspective, from the chaste to the risqué—and charming puns. The first line pointedly references birds and bees doing it, which serves as an extra layer of cleverness given that this is a euphemism for a discussion of sex, while later lyrics note that electric eels are shocked by falling in love. (Rim shot!)

Ella Fitzgerald's "Let's Do It (Let's Fall in Love)" appeared on 1956's *Ella Fitzgerald Sings the Cole Porter Song Book*, an album that later became a Grammy Hall of Fame inductee and member of the Library of Congress's National Recording Registry. Her slow, jazzy version features arrangements and conducting from Buddy Bregman, the nephew of Jule Styne, the legendary composer of songs such as "Let It Snow! Let It Snow! Let It Snow!" and "Diamonds Are a Girl's Best Friend." Fitzgerald plays up the song's mix of whimsy and suggestiveness with a sparkling vocal performance dripping with romance.

"Let's Do It (Let's Fall in Love)" originally appeared in *Paris*, a 1928 musical commissioned by Broadway producer E. Ray Goetz that starred Goetz's wife, Irène Bordoni. At the time of the commission, Porter was still trying to find his place in the songwriting world while playing parties and maintaining a life of luxury in Paris. Incredibly enough, "Let's Do It (Let's Fall in Love)" only made its debut in *Paris* when the musical opened in New York City in October 1928; in pre-premiere productions, a Porter song called "Let's Misbehave" was in its place instead.

The song became one of Porter's first major successes, appearing several years before the composer debuted the beloved musical *Anything Goes* and standards such as "Night and Day" and "It's De-Lovely." But like many love songs, not all of its references have aged well. In early versions of "Let's Do It (Let's Fall in Love)," the first verse featured rather shocking racial slurs. By 1954, however, radio and TV edits of the song replaced these distasteful slurs with mentions of birds and bees. (According to *Billboard*, CBS proposed this lyrical change and NBC accepted it, as did the sheet music company Harms.)

"Let's Do It (Let's Fall in Love)" also appears on the 1957 Louis Armstrong and Ella Fitzgerald album *Ella and Louis Again*, with Armstrong singing the lead. The song has been covered dozens of times across the decades in various genres. Notably, rockers Joan Jett and Paul Westerberg recorded a raucous duet version used as the theme song for the 1995 movie *Tank Girl* that boasts plenty of charm.

IN THE STILL OF THE NIGHT

1956 · THE FIVE SATINS

Songwriter: Fred Parris

EVERY RELATIONSHIP STARTS with a spark—that moment when romance clicks and being together forever seems like a real possibility. Performed by a Connecticut doo-wop group called the Five Satins, "In the Still of the Night" is a snapshot of this spark: two people spending a perfect night together, holding each other and enjoying each other's company.

The narrator pledges eternal fidelity to his beloved, as they're quite certain of their feelings. They're also aware that this precious love isn't guaranteed to last, and so they spend the song fervently wishing for forever. This twist adds a trace of sadness to the music; accordingly, the Five Satins' reverent vocals sound like a solemn prayer for the desired positive outcome.

The Five Satins recorded "In the Still of the Night" with producer Marty Kugell in the basement of St. Bernadette Church in New Haven, Connecticut. (For years, the date of this recording session was reported as December 1955, although more recent articles cite a date of February 19, 1956.) A church altar boy named Vinny Mazzetta connected the group with the space—and, for good measure, also played saxophone on the track. He was joined by a bassist, a drummer, and a pianist, and four of the group's five vocalists, including the song's writer, Fred Parris.

"In the Still of the Night" is based on real-life events. Parris told *Smithsonian* magazine he met the "girl of my dreams," named Marla, in 1954 at a Connecticut amusement park. The couple had a whirlwind romance that led to them becoming engaged; in fact, Marla even moved in with Parris's family.

In the meantime, Parris enlisted in the US Army and was stationed in Philadelphia, away from Marla in Connecticut. After a weekend visit home to see her, he took a train back to the army camp, meditating the whole way on their first meeting and how special their relationship was. "When I arrived at camp, I went straight to the day room," Parris recalled. "There was a piano there and I started playing the chord in my head and the words in my heart." Guard duty soon called, which only added to his introspective mood. "It was a cold, black night, and the stars were twinkling. The setting was very apropos for my feelings and emotions."

Sadly, their romance didn't last. In a cruel twist of fate, that blissful weekend was apparently their last as a couple, as the engagement broke up and Marla eventually moved to California. Nevertheless, the relationship yielded one of the most indelible love songs of all time. Released under the title "In the Still of the Nite" so as not to be confused with a similarly titled Cole Porter tune, the single was warmly reviewed in a June 1956 issue of *Billboard*, which noted the Five Satins "chant with warm expressiveness on a smoothly paced ballad with dramatic lyrics."

The Five Satins' song appeared on the blockbuster soundtrack of 1987's *Dirty Dancing* and is featured prominently at the start of Martin Scorsese's 2019 film *The Irishman*. Ronnie Milsap and the Beach Boys have covered the tune, while Boyz II Men also did a version of the song for the 1992 TV miniseries *The Jacksons: An American Dream*.

FEVER

1958 · PEGGY LEE

Songwriters: Otis Blackwell and Eddie Cooley

WHEN YOU'RE SICK and have a fever, you might feel like you're burning up due to an elevated body temperature. When you're in love, you might also catch a fever—a figurative one, that is, driven by irresistible lust. For proof, just listen to the iconic seduction song "Fever." The lyrics describe sizzling, red-hot romance—the kind of all-consuming attraction that's impossible to ignore. Kissing, touching, happiness—it's all due to the kind of fever that (wink, wink) keeps you up at night and wakes you up in the morning.

"Fever" was co-written by Eddie Cooley and Otis Blackwell. The latter—who also penned Elvis Presley's "Don't Be Cruel" and co-wrote Jerry Lee Lewis's "Great Balls of Fire"—was credited under a pseudonym, John Davenport. "Eddie Cooley was a friend of mine from New York and he called me up and said, 'Man, I got an idea for a song called "Fever," but I can't finish it,'" Blackwell later recalled. "I had to write it under another name because, at that time, I was still under contract to [music publisher] Joe Davis."

The R&B singer Little Willie John recorded "Fever" in 1956, interpreting the song as a swinging blues number with finger snaps, sultry saxophones, and vocal delivery full of longing. His version reached No. 1 on *Billboard*'s R&B Best Sellers chart and Most Played R&B by Jockeys chart—meaning it was a smash on the radio *and* in stores.

Several years later, Peggy Lee took a crack at "Fever." At the time, she was already an established hitmaker, having started her career in the early 1940s as a singer for Benny Goodman and His Orchestra. However, in the time period leading up to her recording the song, she had taken a brief break from performing. "Prior to leaving, she mentioned to me that she was looking for a torch song and that if I heard of anything please let her know," her bassist Max Bennett said in 2001.

He found the right tune during a gig at a Hollywood bar with saxophonist Nino Tempo: A stranger asked to sing "Fever" with the band. "We proceeded to wend our way through the song accompanying him and I realized that it was exactly what Peggy was looking for," Bennett added. "I called Peggy the next day and told her about 'Fever' and she proceeded to find the song."

As Lee prepared for splashy February 1958 shows at the Copacabana in New York City, she worked up "Fever." Her take included new, playful lyrics that invoked the romances of two couples: Romeo and Juliet and Captain Smith and Pocahontas. According to Lee, these added verses were the handiwork of her and a songwriter named Sid Kuller. "I was singing some special lyrics which were partly Sid Kuller's, partly mine, and then of course partly the original song," she told Wink Martindale in an interview dating from the 1970s.

But the sultry, jazzy, stripped-down musical approach—which was dominated by strolling bass and heart-pounding drums—was all her idea. "I was just stomping my foot and snapping my fingers and singing these lyrics to Sammy [Cahn] and he said, 'I think you should do it just that way,' and I said, 'No, I would like to just add bass and drums and that's all.'"

The steady finger snaps, meanwhile, ended up being done by a guitarist who otherwise didn't play on the song, as he'd been "minimalized out of the session because Peg decided this song doesn't need much," the biographer Peter Richmond, who wrote *Fever: The Life and Music of Miss Peggy Lee*, told NPR. "And she was right."

The song became an enormous hit, reaching No. 8 on the *Billboard* Hot 100, and caused a sensation. In August 1958, *Billboard* reported that a DJ for the Boston radio station WILD named Todd O'Hara played the song for 42.5 hours straight. "During the recathon, O'Hara had used up 15 records, received more than 3,000 phone calls and 200 telegrams, mostly favorable, and had scared his brother into thinking he had died with a stuck record going." Lee's "Fever" also had the honor of being nominated for Record of the Year and Best Vocal Performance, Female at the very first Grammy Awards.

Top 10 Romantic Power Ballads

1. Alias, "More Than Words Can Say"
2. Bad English, "When I See You Smile"
3. Celine Dion, "It's All Coming Back to Me Now"
4. Foreigner, "I Want to Know What Love Is"
5. Goo Goo Dolls, "Iris"
6. Heart, "Alone"
7. Lady Gaga, "Yoü and I"
8. Night Ranger, "Sister Christian"
9. REO Speedwagon, "Keep on Lovin' You"
10. Starship, "Nothing's Gonna Stop Us Now"

Dozens of artists have covered "Fever," including Beyoncé, Link Wray, the Cramps, Anne Murray, Danzig, and Ray Charles. Decades later, Lee's version of "Fever" also became a hit yet again—this time on the dance charts—thanks to Madonna, who recorded a seductive house music take for her 1992 album, *Erotica*. This single burned up dance floors across the country as it reached No. 1 on the *Billboard* Hot Dance Club Play chart.

PUT YOUR HEAD ON MY SHOULDER

1959 · PAUL ANKA

Songwriter: Paul Anka

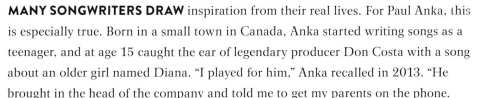

MANY SONGWRITERS DRAW inspiration from their real lives. For Paul Anka, this is especially true. Born in a small town in Canada, Anka started writing songs as a teenager, and at age 15 caught the ear of legendary producer Don Costa with a song about an older girl named Diana. "I played for him," Anka recalled in 2013. "He brought in the head of the company and told me to get my parents on the phone. That week changed my life—they hired me for $100 a week as a singer-songwriter. They wanted me to write and write."

That song, 1957's "Diana," became Anka's breakthrough hit. But in subsequent years, he continued to write songs that captured the exquisite ache of being a teenager—perhaps because he "was going through all these emotions myself," he wrote in his 2013 book, *My Way.* "I was a lonely boy and I knew there were plenty of us out there—I'd see other lonely boys at the hops I'd play. Put your head on my shoulder—that was your objective that weekend . . . plus maybe getting a kiss and your hand in her blouse."

Unsurprisingly, Anka added that "Put Your Head on My Shoulder" grew out of his time playing record hops, which is perhaps why the song so accurately captures the experience of pining for a perfect slow dance. The narrator fantasizes about being physically close to a crush—close enough to exchange whispered sweet nothings and (ideally) a goodnight kiss, which will no doubt lead to a love connection. Anka's vocals exude a mixture of emotions—at times bashful and pleading, at other times saucy and confident—that match the song's puppy-love pleas. And the Costa-directed orchestra and chorus add just the right accompaniment: a pillowy waltzing tempo; sustained guitar licks; and soft, rounded harmonies and background vocals.

Many artists have covered "Put Your Head on My Shoulder," including heartthrob Leif Garrett and vocal group the Lettermen, while Anka dueted with the Chilean performer Myriam Hernández in the late '90s on a Spanish cover called "Tu Cabeza en Mi Hombro." But in 2021, Anka had another unexpected mainstream resurgence when the pop star Doja Cat sampled "Put Your Head on My Shoulder" for her song "Freak." Anka's tune subsequently gained even more notoriety after it became part of a viral phenomenon, mashed up with Doja Cat's "Streets" and used for the TikTok-driven #SilhouetteChallenge. The song was given a modern spin, sampled in all of its innocent glory before fading out and dissolving into Doja Cat's seductive, groove-heavy tune.

I ONLY HAVE EYES FOR YOU

1959 • THE FLAMINGOS

Songwriters: Harry Warren (music); Al Dubin (lyrics)

LOVE CAN BE mesmerizing—so mesmerizing that you can't see anything else but the luminous face of the person you adore. "I Only Have Eyes for You" describes this single-minded focus: The narrator can't see beautiful sights like the stars or the moon—or tell if they're standing in a garden, surrounded by a crowd, or hanging out on a busy street—because they're so absolutely focused on (and head over heels for) their love.

Composer Harry Warren and lyricist Al Dubin wrote "I Only Have Eyes for You" for the 1934 film *Dames*. In the movie, which was codirected by Busby Berkeley, Jimmy Higgens (Dick Powell) sang the tune to performer Barbara (Ruby Keeler) while they were together on a ferry. This jaunty, fully orchestrated version felt frothy and romantic, and suitably full of cinematic drama.

The Flamingos' take on "I Only Have Eyes for You" is dreamy, as if the narrator is mired in a sweet romantic daze, and boasts a unique arrangement built around a waltzing rhythm, doo-wop–inspired vocal flourishes, and an echoing sound effect that translates roughly to *sha-bop-sha-bop*. The new version came from group member Terry "Buzzy" Johnson, who also happened to be a gifted arranger.

In a 2021 interview on the Professor of Rock YouTube channel, Johnson shared that "I Only Have Eyes for You" was the last song recorded for the group's debut album, *Flamingo Serenade*. In fact, he was having trouble figuring out how to make the tune sound better. "It sounds so corny," he said. "I don't like the chord changes."

Johnson tended to practice guitar while lying in bed—and, in a stroke of luck, one night he fell asleep while in a strumming session and started dreaming of a song. "I heard this strange music, but it was beautiful. It was more different than anything I've heard before." At this point in the interview, he sang the song's iconic ringing pattern. "I heard the chord changes, and when it got to the bridge of it, I heard it. And when I woke up, my fingers were on my guitar, and whatever I hit it was exactly what I heard."

According to the song's entry in *Rolling Stone*'s 2021 list of the 500 Greatest Songs of All Time—it ranked at No. 175—Johnson called the rest of the Flamingos right away to capture the song while it was still fresh. "The other members weren't exactly thrilled when he called them over at four in the morning to share his revelation," stated the entry, "but the classic recording proved worth losing a little sleep over." Indeed, the Flamingos' "I Only Have Eyes for You" peaked at No. 11 on the *Billboard* Hot 100 and No. 3 on the magazine's Hot R&B Sides chart. It was later inducted into the Grammy Hall of Fame.

LOVE IS HERE TO STAY

1959 · BILLIE HOLIDAY

Songwriters: George Gershwin (music); Ira Gershwin (lyrics)

IN GOOD TIMES, love is an anchor—something stabilizing that keeps a relationship steady despite choppy waters or other potential disruptions. That's the sweet message conveyed by "Love Is Here to Stay," which cheers on the durability of a romantic bond. The state of the world might be confusing, pop culture is ephemeral, and even (literally) rock-solid landmarks like the Rockies and Gibraltar might collapse one day. In contrast, however, love is permanent *and* forever.

"Love Is Here to Stay" (which is sometimes also called "Our Love Is Here to Stay") was a composition by brothers George and Ira Gershwin that originally appeared in 1938's *The Goldwyn Follies*. At the time, George had moved to Hollywood and was writing music for movies; prior to *The Goldwyn Follies*, he penned songs for the Fred Astaire–Ginger Rogers movie *Shall We Dance* and then the film *A Damsel in Distress*, costarring Astaire, George Burns, and Gracie Allen.

"The screen is a great worldwide medium for music today," the composer told the *Cincinnati Enquirer*. "And it is not difficult to foresee the time when pictures will be using the best efforts of all composers—serious works as well as lighter, popular melodies." His assessment was prescient, although he sadly never saw it come to fruition. In fact, "Love Is Here to Stay" was one of the very last songs George finished before he died in 1937 of a brain tumor.

"Love Is Here to Stay" rose to prominence after appearing in 1951's *An American in Paris*. In an intimate scene, Gene Kelly croons "Love Is Here to Stay" to Leslie Caron as the couple are alone alongside the River Seine. The performance is distinguished by lithe, graceful choreography that reveals the pair's romantic chemistry and the tenderness they have for each other.

Frank Sinatra, Nat King Cole, and Ella Fitzgerald and Louis Armstrong have all covered "Love Is Here to Stay," but the jazzy version by Billie Holiday on her 1959 Verve Records LP *All or Nothing at All* is particularly memorable. For starters, its rhythmic foundation—loping walking bass and whispering drums—is sturdy. Atop this are layers of evocative guitar, fuzzy saxophone, punctuating horns, and piano that sounds like a burbling stream. Holiday's note-perfect vocal performance is the cherry on top: Playful and saucy, her voice sounds like the aural equivalent of twinkling eyes or a flirtatious wink. There's no doubting her intentions—or her commitment to both the song *and* a partner.

WONDERFUL WORLD

1960 · SAM COOKE

Songwriters: Lou Adler, Herb Alpert, Sam Cooke

IN EARLY 1960, Sam Cooke signed a record deal with RCA Victor. His former label Keen issued a single under his name called "Wonderful World." Not to be confused with the Louis Armstrong–popularized "What a Wonderful World," Cooke's song is a sparkling R&B tune with pitter-pattering drums, subtle guitars, and a warm chorus of backing vocalists—all led by Cooke himself, who sounds genteel and pleading as he sings about wooing a crush.

Upon its 1960 release, "Wonderful World" was credited to Barbara Campbell, Cooke's wife. In reality, record producer Lou Adler, A&M Records cofounder Herb Alpert, and Cooke himself co-wrote the tune. Incredibly enough, Adler and Alpert were initially lukewarm on "Wonderful World." In Peter Guralnick's *Dream Boogie: The Triumph of Sam Cooke*, Adler said that Cooke was the driving force in recording the song. "Sam kept coming back to it. He'd say, 'What about that song, you know?' And then he'd start on it again . . . I don't know what it would have been if he didn't get involved, but what it became was because of him."

Cooke's approach was quietly brilliant. The song's narrator says he isn't book-smart but *does* know that he loves someone else—and is convinced that life would be better if those feelings were reciprocated. This concept was also Cooke's idea, Adler shared: "His idea—since it was all about reading and books and what you didn't have to do in order to [find love]—was to take it more towards school."

Indeed, to take the metaphor one step further, "Wonderful World" mentions ignorance of several academic subjects—biology, history, French, trigonometry— *except* the romance-associated math equation $1 + 1 = 2$. Best of all, the narrator is trying to get his grades up into the A-range, since he knows that being smart might make him a more attractive partner. "It was light," Adler said of the song. "It wasn't, 'Listen to this song.' Sam always told me, 'You got to be talking to somebody.'"

"Wonderful World" became a massive hit, reaching No. 12 on the *Billboard* Hot 100 and No. 2 on the Hot R&B Sides chart, and it was also chosen for the Grammy Hall of Fame. In 1965, Herman's Hermits had great success in the US and Canada with a lovelorn cover that featured a pre-fame Jimmy Page on guitar, while Cooke's "Wonderful World" also had a second life after being used in multiple movies. Among other appearances, it can be heard in 1978's *Animal House* and also in the 1985 Harrison Ford–Kelly McGillis film *Witness*. In the UK, "Wonderful World" also reached No. 2 in 1986 after being used in an ad for Levi's jeans.

THIS MAGIC MOMENT

1960 • THE DRIFTERS

Songwriters: Doc Pomus (lyrics); Mort Shuman (music)

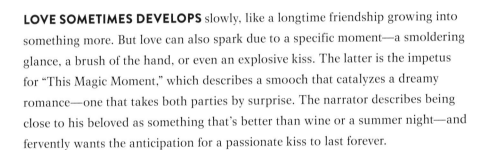

LOVE SOMETIMES DEVELOPS slowly, like a longtime friendship growing into something more. But love can also spark due to a specific moment—a smoldering glance, a brush of the hand, or even an explosive kiss. The latter is the impetus for "This Magic Moment," which describes a smooch that catalyzes a dreamy romance—one that takes both parties by surprise. The narrator describes being close to his beloved as something that's better than wine or a summer night—and fervently wants the anticipation for a passionate kiss to last forever.

Lyricist Doc Pomus—a member of the Rock & Roll Hall of Fame, Songwriters Hall of Fame, and Blues Hall of Fame—and pianist Mort Shuman wrote "This Magic Moment." The men were a dynamic songwriting duo responsible for writing hits such as Dion & the Belmonts' "A Teenager in Love," Elvis Presley's "Viva Las Vegas," and "Save the Last Dance for Me," the latter a hit for New York City troupe the Drifters.

As it so happens, the Drifters were the first group to record "This Magic Moment," in a session that occurred not long after the group had a massive hit with 1959's longing-filled "There Goes My Baby." At this time, the Drifters featured future legend Ben E. King; in fact, he sang lead on "This Magic Moment."

Production, meanwhile, came from the iconic duo Jerry Leiber and Mike Stoller, the men responsible for writing and producing songs like "Hound Dog" and "Jailhouse Rock"—and, later, collaborating with King on his 1961 solo hit "Stand By Me."

"This Magic Moment" was another, well, magical song. After starting with an intro of quivering strings that sound like buzzing bees, the tune then settles into an undulating groove and unfolds slowly, like someone relishing unwrapping a thoughtful gift. Dramatic strings dart back and forth with the delicacy of lithe dancers, alternating between quiet majesty and moments of intensity, while pristine vocal harmonies emphasize certain lyrics in the background. And although he was just in his early 20s, King sounds wise beyond his years—dazzled by his beloved and their budding love.

"This Magic Moment" reached No. 4 on *Billboard*'s Hot R&B Sides chart and peaked at No. 16 on the *Billboard* Hot 100. In 1968, Jay and the Americans had an even bigger hit with their version of the song, a horn-spiced take that charted even higher (No. 6) on the Hot 100. Lou Reed, meanwhile, also contributed a scorching, droning rock version to the soundtrack of David Lynch's 1997 film, *Lost Highway*.

AT LAST

1960 · ETTA JAMES

Songwriters: Mack Gordon and Harry Warren

THERE'S NO BETTER feeling than closing your online dating profile and deleting the apps. That means you've finally found someone with whom you're happy and can stop searching for The One. Co-written by Mack Gordon and Harry Warren— the songwriting team behind "Chattanooga Choo Choo" and the Oscar-winning "You'll Never Know"—"At Last" is the sonic equivalent of that ecstatic feeling.

The song's narrator is on cloud nine because they've found their dream partner, guaranteeing that life is brighter and their loneliness is gone.

"At Last" first appeared several times briefly in *Sun Valley Serenade*, a 1941 movie starring Sonja Henie, John Payne, and Milton Berle, and featured more prominently in the 1942 film *Orchestra Wives*. Incredibly, however, the Glenn Miller and His Orchestra take on "At Last" heard in the latter movie—which featured vocals from Ray Eberle and Pat Friday—almost didn't see the light of day.

According to the July 1942 issue of *Variety*, "At Last" was "salvaged from a cutting room floor. Miller recorded the song for *Sun Valley Serenade* and by the time the editors were through it was not to be found in the picture." But songwriters Warren and Gordon believed in the song and "kept after the studio executives to give the number another try with Miller when the band man was brought back to Hollywood to work in *Wives*." Their instincts were right: A 1942 Glenn Miller and His Orchestra 78 RPM single with Eberle singing "At Last" was a radio favorite, reaching No. 2 on *Billboard*'s Songs with Most Radio Plugs chart.

"At Last" rose to greater fame as the title track of Etta James's 1960 debut album, *At Last!* The artist had experienced some success in the 1950s co-writing and performing a song called "The Wallflower"; among other things, the tune became a *Billboard* R&B chart favorite and led to a stint opening for Little Richard.

"At Last" marked an entirely new chapter for James and became a blueprint for all future love songs. Heralded by majestic strings, the tune blooms into a gorgeous ballad with a subtle slow-dance groove and a stunning vocal performance. James brims with gratitude, her voice rising with excitement as she recalls the night she spotted her beloved and fell *hard*, in no small part because of their amazing smile.

"At Last" became a No. 2 hit on *Billboard*'s Hot R&B Sides chart in 1961 but only reached No. 47 on the overall pop chart. However, the song grew in stature over time. "At Last" was No. 115 on *Rolling Stone*'s 500 Greatest Songs of All Time list in 2021 and was chosen for both the Library of Congress's National Recording Registry and the Grammy Hall of Fame. Over the years, stars such as Joni Mitchell, Stevie Wonder, Beyoncé, and Cyndi Lauper have all covered the tune.

At James's 2012 funeral, Christina Aguilera also performed "At Last" and spoke about why the song means so much to her—and why the vocalist's talent made songs like "At Last" so enduring. "I've aspired to sing like her, to be like her, to emulate her notes and her passion and the love for what she did—I could feel it," Aguilera said. "Out of all the singers I've ever heard, she was the one that cut right to my soul and spoke to me."

I FALL TO PIECES

1961 • PATSY CLINE

Songwriters: Hank Cochran and Harlan Howard

"I FALL TO PIECES" is a stark reminder that the only thing worse than a breakup is encountering your ex again after a breakup. Seeing them brings on a flood of conflicting emotions—happiness, sadness, desperation, regret—as memories of better days mingle with the reminder that you're no longer together. To add insult to injury, it's expected that you're supposed to move on and forget about these good times, even if the thought of being without your ex is too painful. Still, although "I Fall to Pieces" is a deeply sad song, it demonstrates the enduring power of love—and how it keeps a grip on our hearts long after a relationship fizzles out.

The tune was co-written by Hank Cochran and Harlan Howard; the latter also wrote Guy Mitchell's 1959 No. 1 hit "Heartaches by the Number." As recounted in *Honky Tonk Angel: The Intimate Story of Patsy Cline*, the pair built the song around a title Cochran came up with. "Hank arrived around breakfast and we had coffee," Howard said. "He had this song going and sang it with his guitar, 'I fall to pieces, each time I see you again.' And that was about it." Added Cochran: "We wrote it in one of our many down periods, and it was tinged with the right amount of, I guess you could say, hurt and despair."

Howard's wife, the country singer Jan Howard, demoed "I Fall to Pieces" and the legendary country producer Owen Bradley tried to find an artist to cut the tune. Both Brenda Lee and Roy Drusky passed on recording it, and the song ended up on Cline's radar. According to one story, she overheard Drusky declining "I Fall to Pieces" and claimed it for herself after a discussion with Bradley. Other people remember things differently—including Jan Howard, who claimed in *Honky Tonk Angel* that Cline wasn't even a fan of the song. "Let's be more definite," she said. "Patsy hated it. She told me, 'I hate that goddamn song,' knowing full well I was Harlan's wife. That didn't stop her from speaking her mind."

Cline also apparently dragged her feet when it came time for the recording session, with Cochran saying she recorded the song "much against her will" and only after Bradley also allowed her to cut the demo's flipside, "Lovin' in Vain" by Freddie Hart. Still, magic happened once she settled into the studio. Surrounded by top Nashville players—including guitarist Hank Garland, steel guitarist Ben Keith, bassist Bob Moore, keyboardist Hargus "Pig" Robbins, and vocal group the Jordanaires—Cline ended up recording one of her finest vocal parts ever.

Although her voice trembles with emotion, she maintains her composure and sounds strong even while warbling about romantic devastation. "Once Patsy got into the groove, she just caressed those lyrics and that melody so tenderly that it was just like satin," Howard later said. "We knew we had magic in the can when, on the fourth take, every grown man in that studio was bawling like a baby and Bradley said, 'That's the one.'" The instrumentalists support her with tasteful music that sways like a sweet summer breeze.

"I Fall to Pieces" ended up becoming Cline's first hit since 1957's "Walkin' After Midnight." The single peaked at No. 1 for two weeks on *Billboard*'s Hot Country & Western Sides chart and crossed over to the pop charts, reaching No. 12 on the *Billboard* Hot 100. The success allowed her to keep her car from being repossessed and it also kicked off a late-career surge that led to her only top 10 pop hit, the Willie Nelson–penned "Crazy."

Over the years, "I Fall to Pieces" became one of Cline's signature songs. A posthumous version with Jim Reeves made a modest showing on the country charts in 1982, while Aaron Neville and Trisha Yearwood won a Grammy Award for Best Country Collaboration with Vocals with a 1994 cover.

CAN'T HELP FALLING IN LOVE

1961 · ELVIS PRESLEY

Songwriters: Luigi Creatore, Hugo Peretti, George David Weiss

AFTER ELVIS PRESLEY ended his US Army service in 1960, he focused on restarting his movie career. Throughout the 1960s, that meant he acted in two or three films a year. Among the highlights was 1961's *Blue Hawaii*, which found Presley portraying Chad Gates, a soldier-turned-tour guide focused on finding his own way in life with his lovely girlfriend Maile Duval.

In the movie, Presley croons a new song called "Can't Help Falling in Love"—not to Maile, but to her grandmother, after giving her a music box that's playing the tune. The gesture is touching, as it illustrates Gates's respect for his girlfriend's family—and, by extension, his lady.

Lyrically, the protagonist of "Can't Help Falling in Love" is also unabashedly romantic. With poetic aplomb, they confess that they are hopelessly in love and believe the relationship was destined by fate; it's as certain as how a river flows. The magnetic pull of attraction is simply too strong.

Some of music's finest writers and players helped "Can't Help Falling in Love" come to fruition. For starters, the same trio of songwriters also wrote the lyrics to the Tokens' 1961 version of "The Lion Sleeps Tonight" and multiple songs on the Stylistics' 1974 LP *Let's Put It All Together*, while George David Weiss also co-wrote the Louis Armstrong–popularized late-1960s hit "What a Wonderful World."

Presley recorded "Can't Help Falling in Love" on March 23, 1961, with a familiar group of musicians that included vocal group the Jordanaires; guitarists Hank Garland and Scotty Moore; bassist Bob Moore; and drummer D.J. Fontana. Legendary drummer-percussionist Hal Blaine, who also played on Presley hits such as "Return to Sender" and "A Little Less Conversation," also played on the track. Naturally, the song ranks among Presley's best work; it's an earnest lullaby with twilight harmonies, a swaying tempo, and country-tinged instrumentation, all of which complement the King's tenderhearted vocal delivery.

"Can't Help Falling in Love" spent four weeks at No. 1 in the UK and peaked at No. 2 on the US *Billboard* Hot 100. It's now one of Presley's most enduring songs, appearing as part of his *'68 Comeback Special* (as well as several other TV specials) and becoming the last song he ever performed live, in 1977.

Other artists have made the song their own. UB40 gave "Can't Help Falling in Love" the reggae-pop treatment in 1993 for another movie, *Sliver*. This Sharon Stone film certainly wasn't as chaste as *Blue Hawaii*; in fact, the original cut was rated NC-17. And in the 2022 movie *Elvis*, Presley mega-fan Kacey Musgraves performed a bittersweet version of "Can't Help Falling in Love," transforming the song from an optimistic promise to a nostalgic look back.

I CAN'T STOP LOVING YOU

1962 • RAY CHARLES

Songwriter: Don Gibson

>≍ ♥ ≍<

LOVE DOESN'T DISSIPATE immediately when a couple part ways. Sometimes that's by design: After a breakup, many people don't want to let go of romantic feelings, because doing so means accepting that a relationship is over.

The main character of "I Can't Stop Loving You" certainly falls into the latter category. They're not moving on from an ex because they're not yet ready to confront the painful realities of a breakup. Instead, they seek out comfort in loneliness and wallow in shoulda-beens, while lamenting that once-happy memories now make them feel sad. They can't and won't stop loving their ex.

Future Country Music Hall of Fame member Don Gibson wrote "I Can't Stop Loving You" in Knoxville, Tennessee, on the same day he wrote "Oh Lonesome Me," he said in Dorothy Horstman's 1975 book *Sing Your Heart Out, Country Boy.* "I sat down to write a lost love ballad. After writing several lines to the song, I looked back and saw the line 'I can't stop loving you.' I said, 'That would be a good title,' so I went ahead and rewrote it in its present form." The songs emerged during a challenging period of his life; according to his 2003 obituary, both his vacuum cleaner and television had been repossessed recently because his finances were in such bad shape.

Luckily, Gibson struck gold with the song in 1958: Released under the title "I Can't Stop Lovin' You," as a double-sided single with "Oh Lonesome Me," it reached No. 1 on *Billboard*'s Country & Western sales chart. Ray Charles had even more success several years later with a lovelorn, jazzy take on the song, which appeared on his *Modern Sounds in Country and Western Music* LP. The 1962 album is a landmark in the evolution of pop music, as Charles put a modern stamp on country songs—for example, interpreting the Everly Brothers–popularized "Bye Bye Love" as a peppy jazz number.

Recorded at United Recording Studios in Hollywood, on February 15, 1962, "I Can't Stop Loving You" features prominent backing vocals by the Randy Van Horne Singers—the same choral crew heard on theme songs for *The Flintstones* and *The Jetsons*—and swelling string arrangements by noted jazz composer Marty Paich. But the song's true star is Charles. An empathetic narrator, he sounds nostalgic but deeply melancholy, and his sparse piano playing reflects the song's emotional desolation.

In the US, Charles's "I Can't Stop Loving You" was certified gold in 1962, spent five weeks at No. 1 on *Billboard*'s Hot 100 pop chart, and topped the Easy Listening and Hot R&B Sides charts. In the UK, the song was Charles's first and only No. 1 single, spending two weeks atop the chart. Despite such success, Charles wasn't inducted into the Country Music Hall of Fame until 2021.

HEAT WAVE

1963 • MARTHA AND THE VANDELLAS

Songwriters: Brian Holland, Lamont Dozier, Eddie Holland

WHEN YOU'RE AROUND someone to whom you're attracted, your cheeks might flush—or you might get a warm, fuzzy feeling at the mere sight of them. You can't help this reaction: It's involuntary because that's just science (and human nature) talking. Martha and the Vandellas' Motown classic "Heat Wave" captures this sense of sudden desire—and how disorienting it can be—although there's potentially a catch: The narrator is moved to tears by their feelings, maybe because these emotions are overwhelming or perhaps because their crush is unattainable.

Sometimes known as "(Love Is Like a) Heat Wave," the song was written by the legendary songwriting trio Holland–Dozier–Holland; among the hits they penned include "Baby Love," "It's the Same Old Song," "Stop! In the Name of Love," and "You Keep Me Hangin' On." According to Dozier, he wrote the song during a "hot and sticky" period during one Detroit summer. "I often sat at the piano and played a warm-up riff to get my day started," he said. "This one particular day the heat was over the top and I was watching TV and the weatherman said we had a record-breaking five-day heat wave that was not going to let up."

The blazing weather forecast proved to be fertile creative inspiration, Dozier added: "So all this funky riff needed was for me to throw a girl into the mix and this song was born." Of course, the song also needed the right interpreter. Enter Martha Reeves, a vocalist who cut her teeth on gospel and R&B and learned how to perform while singing in Detroit nightclubs.

Backed by the Funk Brothers, the iconic Detroit session musicians who played on plenty of Motown smashes, Reeves was joined by Rosalind Ashford and Annette Beard (original members of Martha and the Vandellas) on vocals. The result is a funky, snappy number that's relentlessly upbeat, courtesy of toe-tapping rhythms, bouncy horns, and the trio's indomitable vocals. Reeves captures the disorienting bliss of the song's big feelings with a powerful performance, while Ashford and Beard bolster the song with ecstatic vocals of their own.

"Heat Wave" was the group's first major hit, as it spent four weeks at No. 1 on the *Billboard* Hot R&B Singles chart and peaked at No. 4 on the *Billboard* Hot 100. The song also earned Motown's first-ever Grammy nomination, for Best Rhythm & Blues Recording, and appeared at No. 257 on the 2021 version of *Rolling Stone*'s 500 Greatest Songs of All Time list.

"Heat Wave" has also appeared in several notable movie scenes. In the 1976 film *Carrie*, the song plays on the radio as the bullies, Billy (John Travolta) and his girlfriend Chris (Nancy Allen), go cruising in a car—a pick that foreshadows their fiery deaths later at the hands of the titular character.

BE MY BABY

1963 · THE RONETTES

Songwriters: Jeff Barry, Ellie Greenwich, Phil Spector

THERE ARE MANY ways to ask someone to go steady. The old-fashioned way involved receiving your crush's class ring, which you'd proudly wear at school for everyone to see. In this modern world, you might have a mature, adult conversation about your relationship—and then mutually decide to delete your dating apps. But perhaps the most timeless and romantic way to make your relationship official is through song. In fact, the Ronettes' "Be My Baby" is perfect for this gesture. The lyrics dole out compliments, promise tons of affection, and predict that the subject of the song would make a beautiful partner. For good measure, the title is repeated throughout the lyrics in the form of a question—as if by using repetition, they'll convince the other person to say yes.

"Be My Baby" was co-written by Phil Spector, Jeff Barry, and Ellie Greenwich in Phil's office on 62nd Street. The Ronettes also rehearsed the song in New York, Ronnie Spector told *The Guardian*. But recording took place at Gold Star Studios in California as part of a recording session spread out over multiple days—"It took three days to record my vocals, take after take," Ronnie recalled—after she flew out west by herself to sing. "My mom usually flew with me but because it was so far she said,

'Honey, you're 18. You can do this on your own now.' Phil picked me up at the airport and kept saying, 'This record is going to be amazing.'"

Musically, "Be My Baby" just might be one of the most influential songs of all time. It starts with an oft-mimicked drum pattern from Hal Blaine that sounds like the pitter-patter of a heart skipping a beat. "That famous drum intro was an accident," Blaine told *The Guardian*. "I was supposed to play the snare on the second beat as well as the fourth, but I dropped a stick. Being the faker I was in those days, I left the mistake in and it became: 'Bum-ba-bum-BOOM!'"

The recording augments Blaine's part with lush contributions from multiple members of famed session group the Wrecking Crew—including bassist Carol Kaye and keyboardist Leon Russell—snaky grooves, and graceful, spinning strings; in fact, it was the first time Phil recorded strings at Gold Star. "I love those strings, particularly at the end," engineer Larry Levine told *Sound on Sound*. "They made me cry when I was mixing."

For her longing-filled vocal performance, Ronnie took inspiration from her Frankie Lymon albums and the experience of being so far away from home. "The recording captures the full spectrum of my emotions: everything from nervousness to excitement," she told *The Guardian*. "When I came in with 'The night we met I knew I needed you so,' the band went nuts. I was 18 years old, 3,000 miles from home, and had all these guys saying I was the next Billie Holliday [*sic*]."

Rounding things out was a kaleidoscopic chorus of backing vocalists, which contributed spectral harmonies. As Ronnie recalled in her book *Be My Baby*, that part of the session drew a crowd. "Darlene Love was there, and we had Fanita James from the Blossoms, Bobby Sheen from Bob B. Soxx and the Blue Jeans, Nino Tempo, Sonny Bono—who was Phil's gofer in those days—and Sonny's girlfriend, who was a gawky teenager named Cher."

"Be My Baby" became a massive hit for the Ronettes, reaching No. 2 on the *Billboard* Hot 100 and No. 4 on the Hot R&B Singles chart. The song's impact on popular music is difficult to overstate. Blaine's drum opening has been mimicked on hundreds of songs, while the lush, enveloping instrumentation had a massive influence on Beach Boys genius Brian Wilson.

"Brian must have played 'Be My Baby' ten million times," Beach Boys member Bruce Johnston said in Mick Brown's book *Tearing Down the Wall of Sound: The Rise and Fall of Phil Spector*. "He never seemed to get tired of it." Wilson was so inspired by the song, in fact, that he wrote "Don't Worry Baby"—which became a signature Beach Boys hit—and started hiring the Wrecking Crew to play on records.

FLY ME TO THE MOON

1964 • FRANK SINATRA

Songwriter: Bart Howard

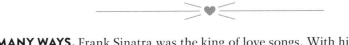

IN MANY WAYS, Frank Sinatra was the king of love songs. With his snazzy demeanor and sophisticated vocal delivery, the Chairman of the Board was a smooth operator who brought panache and romance to the Great American Songbook.

One of his finest moments is an extroverted version of "Fly Me to the Moon," a timeless ode to being completely smitten with someone else. Found on Sinatra's 1964 LP with Count Basie and His Orchestra, *It Might As Well Be Swing*, the tune captures the soaring, out-of-this-world feeling that comes from expressing your love and affection. Musically, it's note-perfect jazz with brass accents and vibrant dynamics that features arrangements by none other than Quincy Jones.

"Fly Me to the Moon" was written by Bart Howard. A native of Burlington, Iowa, Howard found fame and fortune in New York City as an accompanist, including at the legendary Rainbow Room. Howard's career crested during the 1950s when he was the emcee and a pianist at New York City nightclub the Blue

Angel. In 1954, a cabaret singer named Felicia Sanders introduced a Howard composition called "Fly Me to the Moon," which was originally known as "In Other Words." Later that same year, Kaye Ballard recorded the song.

Years later, "Fly Me to the Moon" finally reached a wider audience, when Peggy Lee performed a rather delicate take on *The Ed Sullivan Show* in 1960 while walking in front of a backdrop portraying a beatific ocean. In early 1963, the composer and pianist Joe Harnell and his orchestra landed in the top 20 of the *Billboard* Hot 100 with another version of the song dubbed "Fly Me to the Moon—Bossa Nova." That version won a Grammy Award for Best Performance by an Orchestra—For Dancing, and was also up for Record of the Year.

"Fly Me to the Moon" also benefited from great timing. NASA adopted the song for various celebrations once the space program took off in the 1960s. In fact, the astronauts on the May 1969 Apollo 10 mission—a mission that occurred mere months before the first men landed on the moon—jokingly played Sinatra's version of the song during a TV broadcast from space. "This is just so that you guys don't get too excited about the TV and forget what your job is down there," pilot Gene Cernan told the crew back on Earth before hitting play on a mixtape with the song. Fittingly, decades later, NASA hired Diana Krall to perform "Fly Me to the Moon" during a 40th anniversary celebration of the 1969 moon landing.

Howard felt vindicated by all the success, as he told the *New York Times* in 1988. "I've always said it took me 20 years to find out how to write a song in 20 minutes. The song just fell out of me. One publisher wanted me to change the lyric to 'take me to the moon.' Had I done that I don't know where I'd be today." He was inducted into the Songwriters Hall of Fame in 1999.

MY GIRL

1964 • THE TEMPTATIONS

Songwriters: Smokey Robinson and Ronald White

IT'S IMPOSSIBLE TO miss the parallels between Mary Wells's "My Guy" and the Temptations' "My Girl." That's almost certainly because Smokey Robinson had a hand in writing both songs. Just like in "My Guy," the narrator of "My Girl" uses clever imagery to describe deep loyalty toward a partner; here, the bees are jealous that he has an abundance of honey, aka a sweet lady. And musically, the lush backdrop provided by the Funk Brothers and the Detroit Symphony Orchestra is starry-eyed and optimistic—highlighted by the way a dramatic, burbling bass defers to glorious strings and celebratory multi-part harmonies from the Temptations.

"There are no new words," Robinson said in 2020 on the *Rolling Stone Music Now* podcast. "There are no new notes. My thoughts as a songwriter have always been this: 'How can I say "I love you" in a way like it's never been said?'"

For starters, Robinson envisioned a different voice expressing such sentiments. Most notably, "My Girl" was the first Temptations hit to feature baritone David Ruffin on lead vocals; previously, the tenor Eddie Kendricks was the most prominent voice. This swap was by design, Robinson told NPR in 2000. "All I needed was the right song for his voice and I felt like I would have a smash hit record. So I sat down at the piano to write a song for David Ruffin's voice. So I wanted to make it something that he could belt out, but yet make it melodic and sweet." Ruffin indeed was an inspired choice, as his warm-syrup delivery and falsetto croon are romantic.

Robinson wrote "My Girl" while touring as part of the Motortown Revue, a multi-artist package that featured Motown's biggest stars. The song was actually a collaboration with the Temptations; in fact, he vividly recalled working out

Top 10 Wedding First Dance Songs

1. Louis Armstrong, "What a Wonderful World"
2. Bright Eyes, "First Day of My Life"
3. Ben Folds, "The Luckiest"
4. Etta James, "At Last"
5. Norah Jones, "Come Away with Me"
6. Ben E. King, "Stand by Me"
7. John Legend, "All of Me"
8. Bruno Mars, "Marry You"
9. Ed Sheeran, "Thinking Out Loud"
10. Taylor Swift, "Lover"

"My Girl" with the group at the Apollo Theater. "I was just showing David Ruffin how to sing 'My Girl' or the melody and [how] I thought how he should interpret it, and they would be over standing on the side of the piano making up the background vocals."

Recorded in Detroit in late 1964, "My Girl" became the group's first No. 1 pop hit in March 1965 and spent six weeks atop *Billboard*'s Hot Rhythm & Blues Singles chart. Motown head Berry Gordy *knew* the song would become a big hit and even gave Robinson his $1,000 bonus for producing the song well in advance. "He called me into his office and he said, 'Hey, man, I want to give you your producer's bonus check,'" Robinson told NPR, noting that he asked Gordy which song the bonus was for. His response? "My Girl" by the Temptations. "[Gordy] said, 'It's not number one yet, but it's most definitely going there.'"

The song's musical impact had a long tail, however. Otis Redding had a UK hit with his 1965 version of "My Girl," while artists such as Dolly Parton, the Rolling Stones, and Marvin Gaye also recorded covers. In 1985, Daryl Hall and John Oates even reached No. 20 on the *Billboard* Hot 100 with a version of "The Way You Do the Things You Do/My Girl" recorded live with David Ruffin and Eddie Kendricks.

"My Girl" also became a staple of movies, providing the title of a 1991 cult favorite starring Macaulay Culkin and Anna Chlumsky, and appearing in 1983's *The Big Chill* and 1989's *Born on the Fourth of July*. In honor of its enduring popularity, "My Girl" was inducted into the Library of Congress's National Recording Registry and ended up at No. 43 on *Rolling Stone*'s 500 Greatest Songs of All Time list in 2021.

MY GUY

1964 · MARY WELLS

Songwriter: Smokey Robinson

MARY WELLS WAS one of Motown's earliest stars. Signed to the label when she was still a teenager, she earned multiple top 10 pop hits in the early 1960s, thanks to a trio of songs written (or co-written) by Smokey Robinson: "Two Lovers" and "You Beat Me to the Punch"—both of which also reached No. 1 on *Billboard*'s R&B Singles chart—and "The One Who Really Loves You."

In the 2012 book *Mary Wells: The Tumultuous Life of Motown's First Superstar*, Brenda Holloway, who was also signed to Motown in the early 1960s, shared the sentiment around the label about Mary. "She's an untouchable, because she's the one with all the hits. We were wannabees. We were trying to be her. Everything she touched . . . turned to gold. She was Miss Motown."

Wells gained even more fame in 1964 thanks to another Robinson tune, "My Guy," which spent two weeks at No. 1 on the *Billboard* Hot 100—making it the very first chart-topping song for the Motown Records label—and No. 5 in the UK. (In fact, it was also Motown's first hit in England.) Narrated by a joyful girlfriend who can't stop gushing about the greatness of her boyfriend, "My Guy" is an aspirational tune about achieving a rock-solid relationship. *Nothing* can tear them apart, she stresses—and she couldn't be more satisfied.

What was the secret to the song's success? First and foremost, the "My Guy" lyrics are fanciful, with bouncy rhymes at the ends of lines and unique ways of describing fidelity; for example, the narrator describes their solid bond as if she were a stamp glued to a letter. Plus, she admits the guy in question isn't perfect—but he's perfect *for her*, which is vastly more important.

Musically, "My Guy" is also special—romantic and earnest and brimming with heart and genuine emotion. Produced by Robinson, the easygoing tune was recorded with Motown house band the Funk Brothers—a group that included bassist James Jamerson and keyboardist Earl Van Dyke—and backing vocalists the Andantes. As a result, "My Guy" boasts a swaying tempo, snapping rhythms, welcoming harmonies, and crisp horns, as well as some distinctive signifiers. The very beginning interpolates a brief snippet of "Canadian Sunset," a song popularized by jazz pianist Eddie Heywood and composer Hugo Winterhalter in the late 1950s, while Wells decided to channel Hollywood legend Mae West as the song ends. Unsurprisingly, "My Guy" was inducted into the Grammy Hall of Fame in 1999.

UNCHAINED MELODY

1965 • THE RIGHTEOUS BROTHERS

Songwriters: Alex North (music); Hy Zaret (lyrics)

LOVE ISN'T ALWAYS sunshine and rainbows, especially if you're separated from someone you adore. In those moments, distance makes it agonizingly impossible to have the only thing you want: to hold and be close to the person you love. All you can do is ask them to wait for you—and hope their patience doesn't run out.

"Unchained Melody," which was written for a little-remembered 1955 movie called *Unchained*, precisely captures those times when love becomes physically and emotionally painful. As it turns out, the song almost didn't happen: When composer Alex North rang up Hy Zaret to hire him to write lyrics, Zaret initially rebuffed him because he was otherwise occupied—painting his house. But the lyricist managed to find time to scribble some words to go along with the melancholy music.

"Unchained Melody" ended up becoming an almost instant standard. A huge hit that year, it topped *Billboard*'s Honor Roll of Hits, earned an Oscar nomination for Best Original Song, and spawned multiple covers. Although the crooning version by onetime Duke Ellington vocalist Al Hibbler was perhaps most successful—it also topped the *Cash Box* singles chart—takes by Les Baxter and Roy Hamilton were also popular, joining versions by (among others) Liberace, Chet Atkins, and Guy Lombardo and His Royal Canadians. "Unchained Melody" was even more of a phenomenon in the UK: During the chart week starting June 16, 1955, there were a whopping four separate versions in the top 20 of the singles chart.

A decade later, "Unchained Melody" leaped to even greater infamy when the Righteous Brothers—the duo of Bill Medley and Bobby Hatfield—covered the tune. Draped with gauzy orchestral flourishes and driven by Hatfield's trembling tenor, this version oozes longing and feels like a throwback to the early days of rock 'n' roll. Issued by Phil Spector's label Phillies Records, "Unchained Melody" wasn't positioned to be a hit. Medley disclosed in his memoir, *The Time of My Life: A Righteous Brother's Memoir*, that Spector liked to put songs he deemed terrible on the B-side of singles so these tunes wouldn't receive airplay. Inexplicably, that meant "Unchained Melody" was on the flipside of a tune called "Hung on You."

To Medley's additional irritation, the single label deliberately incorrectly stated that Spector—not Medley—produced the song. "I even played the Wurlitzer piano on the cut," Medley wrote. "Believe me, if I thought it was going to be a hit I'd have hired a real piano player." When "Unchained Melody" did start taking off, Spector even tried to sabotage the single's success, calling radio stations and asking them to *stop* playing the tune. But momentum was on the Righteous Brothers' side: The song reached No. 4 on the *Billboard* Hot 100.

The Righteous Brothers rerecorded "Unchained Melody" in 1990, when the original song surged into pop culture once again after appearing in the Patrick Swayze–Demi Moore romance, *Ghost*. This version reached No. 19 on the *Billboard* Hot 100 and even received a Grammy nomination for Best Pop Performance by a Duo or Group with Vocal. "Unchained Melody" has since remained a favorite song to cover. In 1999, the American Society of Composers, Authors and Publishers (ASCAP) included "Unchained Melody" on its list of the 25 most-performed songs/musical works of the 20th century. And the Songwriters Hall of Fame gave "Unchained Melody" its Towering Song award—an honor bestowed on only the most iconic, enduring music.

I GOT YOU BABE

1965 · SONNY AND CHER

Songwriter: Sonny Bono

IS THERE ANYTHING sexier than a partner who says they have your back in *any* situation? Rhetorical question—*definitely* not. That's one reason why "I Got You Babe" by Sonny and Cher—no last names needed—is so renowned. In the lyrics, the singers (who were a couple in real life) talk about supporting each other in the face of skeptics, bringing comfort to their partner in scary situations, and cheering each other up in sad times. All they need to do is hold hands—and the world is their oyster.

Sonny and Cher came by their us-against-the-world mentality honestly. "We looked different than anyone else," Cher told *Billboard* in 2015. "We got thrown out of every place." This was no hyperbole: In 1966, she told the *New Musical Express* that Bono wrote "I Got You Babe" after a Los Angeles restaurant kicked them out because of what they were wearing.

In the same interview, Bono earnestly added, "I know what it is like to see the girl you love hurt because a hotel refuses you admission because of your dress. I know what it is like to have that one person stand by you. There are a lot of other people who have experienced these things and I'm trying to put our feelings into words for everyone."

Bono composed "I Got You Babe" on the couple's well-loved, well-worn $85 piano. (In her book *The First Time*, Cher quoted Bono as noting, "It's only got three broken keys, and they're all down in the

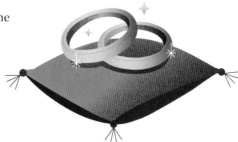

bass end, where we don't sing.") As was his creative preference, he wrote the lyrics on a piece of cardboard.

Cher admitted to *Billboard* she was "never a very good barometer" of a classic song. In fact, she was rather ambivalent about "I Got You Babe" when she first heard the song. "Sonny woke me up in the middle of the night to come in where the piano was, in the living room, and sing it," Cher said. "And I didn't like it and just said, 'OK, I'll sing it and then I'm going back to bed.'" Later, she eventually warmed to the song after Bono modified the bridge to include a modulation, or a key change.

Sonny and Cher recorded the song with an impressive group that included members of the famed Wrecking Crew (to name a few, guitarist Barney Kessel, bassist Lyle Ritz, pianist Don Randi) and musicians in the Herb Alpert–formed Baja Marimba Band (leader Julius Wechter, guitarist Ervan Coleman). As a result, the waltzing song is lush, twinkling '60s pop, albeit with a twist: The rollicking harpsichord from Michel Rubini (also a member of the Wrecking Crew) and Warren Webb's peppy oboe give "I Got You Babe" a distinctive sound.

Over time, there have been a few notable covers of "I Got You Babe," including an undulating, reggae-influenced 1985 take pairing the UK band UB40 and Pretenders leader Chrissie Hynde; this version reached No. 1 on the UK singles chart and reached the top 40 of the *Billboard* Hot 100.

In 1993, Cher also rerecorded "I Got You Babe" with the hapless-but-loveable cartoon characters Beavis and Butt-Head. Incredibly enough, this version reached the UK top 40 and was even a top 10 hit in the Netherlands. Amusingly, in the movie *Groundhog Day*, Sonny and Cher's "I Got You Babe" was also the alarm clock music that woke up Bill Murray's grouchy character Phil Connors day after day.

Although Sonny and Cher's professional partnership eventually dissipated in the 1970s, the pair did perform the song together in 1987—for what would be the last time—on *Late Night with David Letterman*. Poignantly, after Bono's 1998 death in a skiing accident, the very first time Cher performed the song again was in 2002 with the rock band R.E.M., who had covered "I Got You Babe" as far back as 1983.

GOD ONLY KNOWS

1966 · THE BEACH BOYS

Songwriters: Tony Asher and Brian Wilson

YOU KNOW YOU'VE written a timeless tune when Paul McCartney can't say enough great things about your work. Just ask Brian Wilson of the Beach Boys, co-writer of the spectral "God Only Knows," a fond appreciation of a partner and a highlight of the band's influential *Pet Sounds*.

"'God Only Knows' is one of the few songs that reduces me to tears every time I hear it," McCartney told BBC Radio 1 in 2007. "It's really just a love song, but it's brilliantly done. It shows the genius of Brian." The Beatle added that when he had a chance to perform "God Only Knows" with Wilson, it was a deeply emotional experience: "I'm afraid to say that during the sound check I broke down."

So what makes "God Only Knows" so moving? First and foremost, the narrator comes across as innocent and is clearly in awe of their partner's kindness and generosity. But they're also blunt about their feelings: If the couple ever parted ways, life would be much dimmer and possibly not worth living. And so above all, the narrator is grateful for the companionship and romance—a simple but powerful emotion that speaks volumes.

Wilson told *The Guardian* in 2015 that he and Tony Asher wrote the song in 45 minutes. Asher confirmed this account to *Rolling Stone*, noting the song "came pretty quickly. And Brian spent a lot of time working on what ended up being the instrumental parts of that song. But the part that has lyrics really was one of those things that just kinda came out as a whole."

Musically, "God Only Knows" embodies the lush, adventurous music heard on *Pet Sounds*—after all, instruments used on the song include plastic orange juice cups (for percussion) and a tack piano with the strings taped, as well as traditional fare such as a French horn and flute. With cinematic accompaniment from studio musicians the Wrecking Crew and honeyed lead vocals by the late Carl Wilson—"I said my brother Carl will probably be able to impart the message better than I could, so I sacrificed that one," Brian once said—"God Only Knows" feels like a portal to a magical dreamworld.

There was potentially another good reason "God Only Knows" is so spellbinding, Wilson told the *Denver Post* in 2015—and it has to do with a certain Beatles album and some recreational substances. "I listened to *Rubber Soul* and smoked some marijuana and was so blown away that I went right over to my piano and wrote 'God Only Knows' with a friend of mine."

Today, the song is considered one of Brian Wilson's masterpieces, with covers done by a variety of artists, including Neil Diamond, Olivia Newton-John, Glen Campbell, David Bowie, Taylor Swift, and R.E.M.'s Michael Stipe.

I'M A BELIEVER

1966 • THE MONKEES

Songwriter: Neil Diamond

THE MONKEES WERE one of the most improbable bands of the 1960s—a quartet that grew from a fictional group starring on a TV show into a full-fledged, real-life phenomenon that sold millions of records. Among their most famous songs is the well-crafted pop gem "I'm a Believer."

Buoyed by instrumental flourishes from a bevy of ace session musicians, the laid-back song feels like a warm pastiche of '60s popular music: sun-kissed California pop, gritty garage rock, and Beatles-esque melodic rock. Fittingly, the song is about how one moment can turn your love life around. The narrator is initially deeply cynical about romance. They not only can't find the right person, they've also been emotionally wounded by unlucky relationships. But after catching a glimpse of someone's beautiful face, the protagonist falls head over heels in love. Their heart melts, their skepticism falls away, and they go all-in on romantic bliss.

"I'm a Believer" was produced by Jeff Barry, who was responsible for countless 1960s Motown and pop hits in collaboration with songwriting partner Ellie Greenwich. Micky Dolenz took lead vocals, and Davy Jones and Peter Tork contributed backing vocals. The fourth Monkee, Michael Nesmith, ended up being MIA on the track due to musical disagreements. "[He had] a big attitude right from the beginning, and he said at one point, 'I'm a producer too, and that ain't no hit,'" Barry said in the liner notes of a 2006 reissue of *More of the Monkees*.

Today, Nesmith's reaction seems off base, especially when you consider that the now legendary Neil Diamond wrote "I'm a Believer." In late 1966, however, Diamond was a fledgling new artist who had just released his first full-length album, *The Feel of Neil Diamond*—and "I'm a Believer" was simply another song in his arsenal waiting to be recorded. "It just was a little simple kind of self-expression thing," he said in the *More of the Monkees* liner notes. "[A] happy kind of thing. I didn't think too much of it. I just liked the title—that's how the song came."

Lucky for Diamond, however, *The Feel of Neil Diamond* produced a top 10 US hit in the upbeat, feel-good "Cherry, Cherry." The tune caught the ear of none other than Monkees TV show music supervisor Don Kirshner, who decided a song in that vein would also be perfect for the band. Kirshner called up Barry and Greenwich (who happened to work with Diamond) and asked if the young songwriter had any more gems. In the end, the team earmarked three Diamond tunes for the Monkees—including "I'm a Believer."

The song seemed destined to become a hit. An ad in the December 3, 1966, issue of *Billboard* touted, "1,051,280 ordered before release!" of the single, which was backed by the B-side "(I'm Not Your) Steppin' Stone." *Billboard* helped the single's cause with a glowing review that dubbed the record as having "two blockbuster sides that will hit with immediate impact," with "I'm a Believer" especially coming across as "an easy-go dance mover."

Perhaps even more important, the song appeared on the Monkees' popular weekly TV show. For example, during the December 12 episode, "Dance, Monkee, Dance"—which involved the band members using both wily charms and slapstick antics to counteract the sketchy dealings of a dance studio—"I'm a Believer" appears prominently during a crucial denouement scene. By the December 31, 1966, issue of *Billboard*, the song had reached No. 1 on the Hot 100, a position it held for seven weeks overall. In the UK, it was also a smash, spending four weeks atop the singles chart.

Diamond played guitar on the Monkees hit and also cut "I'm a Believer" himself in 1967. Younger generations have also come to know and love the song thanks to covers by Smash Mouth and Weezer. The former introduced "I'm a Believer" to entirely new fans after recording a kicky, organ-driven cover for the 2001 movie cartoon *Shrek*; this version reached No. 25 on *Billboard*'s Hot 100 and was popular in Spain, Australia, and New Zealand. Weezer, meanwhile, tapped into the song's guitar-heavy power-pop side for their own take for 2010's *Shrek Forever After*.

TRY A LITTLE TENDERNESS

1966 · OTIS REDDING

Songwriters: Jimmy Campbell, Reg Connelly, Harry M. Woods

ON DECEMBER 9, 1967, Otis Redding appeared on the Cleveland, Ohio, TV show *Upbeat* and performed "Try a Little Tenderness." The song had been a pop and R&B hit earlier in the year. Although slightly constrained by the small TV stage, he was animated and passionate, letting the music wash over him as if he was infused with the Holy Spirit. It's a mesmerizing, moving version that illuminates his charismatic stage presence and inimitable voice.

Tragically, the very next day after their appearance, Redding and his band died in a plane crash, cutting short a promising career that was on an upswing. (Posthumously, he had a massive hit in early 1968 with the indelible "(Sittin' on) the Dock of the Bay," which spent four weeks at No. 1 on the *Billboard* Hot 100.) "Try a Little Tenderness"—a song that encourages compassion, understanding, and a gentle touch when dealing with a lady—is certainly another one of his greatest legacies.

Redding recorded "Try a Little Tenderness" at the urging of his manager, Phil Walden. "I remember he called me late at night and he said, 'You know that song you've been on my ass about recording, "Try a Little Tenderness"?'" Walden said in *Soulsville, U.S.A.: The Story of Stax Records*. "I said, 'Yeah.' He said, 'I cut that motherfucker. It's a brand-new song.' He could just turn things around, he could hear it in such a different way."

Indeed, Redding's take is a marvel of dynamics and instrumental restraint. Backed by Booker T. & the M.G.'s and featuring arrangements by Isaac Hayes and contributions from the Mar-Key horns, "Try a Little Tenderness" begins like a solemn church hymn and evolves into a cathartic soul number. To achieve this effect, drummer Al Jackson Jr. kept his rhythms minimal until the song was already well underway.

"Otis just took that and ran with it," Booker T. said in *Soulsville, U.S.A.* "He really got excited once he found out what Al was going to do on the drums. He realized how he could finish the song. That he could start it like a ballad and finish it full of emotion."

"Try a Little Tenderness" was actually written by Jimmy Campbell, Reg Connelly, and Harry M. Woods decades before Redding recorded the tune. It was also originally conceived as a jaunty orchestral croon; in fact, two orchestras cut versions of the song in 1932, the same year it was registered with the US Copyright Office. The following year, both Ted Lewis and Ruth Etting recorded well-received versions of the song that tugged at people's heartstrings.

In a 1933 *Charlotte Observer* column, the writer Elsie Robinson even dissected the song line by line, tapping into the tune's gentle optimism: "Tomorrow—next week—you'd tell her how you loved her. And now it's too late. Or is it? Isn't there still a chance? If you phoned her now—wrote her that little note—couldn't you, maybe, start all over again?"

In subsequent years, both Frank Sinatra and Bing Crosby recorded "Try a Little Tenderness." But Booker T. & the M.G.'s guitarist Steve Cropper noted that Redding and the musicians were inspired by other renditions of the song: a 1962 version by Aretha Franklin and a 1964 live take by Sam Cooke. Both of these versions sounded more genuine and empathetic—two traits Redding incorporated, and then some, on his version.

Over the years, Redding's take has become the most well-known version of the song. In the 1986 movie *Pretty in Pink*, record store proprietor Iona (Annie Potts) drops the needle on "Try a Little Tenderness." The song inspires Duckie (Jon Cryer) to do an exaggerated interpretive dance all around the store in an attempt to impress his love interest, Andie (Molly Ringwald). And on the 2011 collaborative album *Watch the Throne*, Jay-Z and Kanye West sampled and incorporated Redding's song for their own composition, "Otis."

WHEN A MAN LOVES A WOMAN

1966 • PERCY SLEDGE

Songwriters: Andrew Wright (music); Calvin Lewis (lyrics)

PERCY SLEDGE'S "When a Man Loves a Woman" offers some hard truths about being in love. For starters, it's not out of the ordinary to see your relationship through rose-colored glasses and ignore red flags, like being treated unfairly by your partner. (If anything, everyone *else* sees any poor behavior before you do.)

Being in love can also make you do all sorts of out-of-character things: jettison your best friend if they insult your lady, say, or sleep outside when it's raining because she wants you to. You're simply so infatuated with your partner that you excuse (and sacrifice) many things.

Growing up in Alabama, Sledge sang with a group called the Esquires, although he didn't necessarily see music as a professional path; in fact, he was considering professional sports instead. Despite this experience, Sledge considered "When a Man Loves a Woman" a sonic departure, he told *Blues & Soul* magazine in 1970. "In high school, I was into this group scene with the bass and soprano and all that. Then, when I left school, I completely gave up singing and people kept encouraging me to start singing and to cut records. So the next thing I know, I'm singing 'When a Man Loves a Woman' and it was completely different from what I had been used to singing."

According to Jimmy Johnson, the engineer who recorded Sledge's history-making vocal performance at Norala Sound Studio on February 17, 1966, that fresh start made a difference. "At that time Percy had never sung on a record before. And the performance he gave was so pristine and so good that it was almost hard to believe that was his first time." Indeed, Sledge's velvet-textured performance is stunning—unselfconscious, aching, and from the heart, and infused with longing and desire. Near the end of the song, Sledge practically beseeches his lady to be kind and treat him well.

As it turns out, Sledge might have been familiar with "When a Man Loves a Woman" long before recording it: In an interview with the Rock & Roll Hall of Fame, Sledge noted, "I hummed it all my life, even when I was picking and chopping cotton in the fields." That same Rock Hall piece noted that Sledge came up with some of the lyrics on the fly during a University of Mississippi frat party appearance—and the song was originally titled "Why Did You Leave Me, Baby?" as Sledge drew on a painful experience where a girl left him for someone else.

The tune's credited co-writers are two of Sledge's Esquires bandmates, bassist Cameron Lewis and organist Andrew Wright; in another telling of the origin story, they alone are responsible for the song. "We were set to play a Friday night dance, and we were practicing," Wright told *American Songwriter* in 1994. "I was messing around on the organ when this riff came up out of nowhere. There was no one in the club but us. I told Calvin to go home and write some words." Their fresh composition was "going to be Percy's audition for producers in town," Wright added. "The only one who would listen was Quin Ivy."

Ivy just so happened to own Norala Sound Studio, where Sledge recorded "When a Man Loves a Woman" alongside a crew of legendary area musicians: Spooner Oldham on Farfisa organ, bassist Albert Lowe, drummer Roger Hawkins, and a 15-year-old backup singer named Doris Allen. Later, the song's co-producer, Marlin Greene, contributed guitar, horns, and background vocals.

The resulting single landed in front of Jerry Wexler of Atlantic Records. The label released "When a Man Loves a Woman," and the single became a huge hit, reaching No. 1 on *Billboard*'s Hot 100 and Top Selling R&B Singles charts. Crooner Michael Bolton also topped the pop charts (and the *Billboard* Hot Adult Contemporary chart) with a 1991 cover of the song that earned him a Grammy Award for Best Male Pop Vocal Performance.

(YOU MAKE ME FEEL LIKE) A NATURAL WOMAN

1967 • ARETHA FRANKLIN

Songwriters: Gerry Goffin, Carole King, Jerry Wexler

WHEN YOU'RE WITH the right partner, they bring out the best in you. Their presence makes you feel grounded and positive, and you feel ready to face the day and handle whatever challenges are in store. That's the sweet message driving "(You Make Me Feel Like) A Natural Woman." Released initially under the title "A Natural Woman," the song describes how nice it feels to be with someone who amplifies the best parts of yourself and helps you feel less lost in this big, wide world.

Soul great Aretha Franklin performed the most famous version of "(You Make Me Feel Like) A Natural Woman." Found on the 1968 LP *Lady Soul*, the strings-swirled song features legendary instrumentalists (bassist Tommy Cogbill, drummer Gene Chrisman) and backing vocals from the Sweet Inspirations and Franklin's sisters, Carolyn and Erma Franklin. Aretha herself gives a career-highlight performance that exudes gratitude and longing, as if the other person has rescued her from a dreary life. The resulting music feels like the highlight of a church service—the kind of celebratory song playing when a congregation is finally able to commemorate salvation.

If the tune sounded tailor-made for Franklin, there was a very good reason for it. Carole King and Gerry Goffin wrote "(You Make Me Feel Like) A Natural Woman" in 1967. The couple, married at the time, were walking on Broadway in Manhattan and encountered Atlantic Records' Jerry Wexler riding in a limousine. The executive rolled down the window so he could relay a message from the car, King told the *New Yorker* in 2016: "[He said] 'I'm looking for a really big hit for Aretha. How about writing a song called "A Natural Woman"?'"

Inspired, King and Goffin started brainstorming ideas all the way home to their house in New Jersey and wrote "(You Make Me Feel Like) A Natural Woman" that very night after their kids had gone to bed. "I sat down at the piano, put my hands on the keys, and played a few chords," King wrote in her 2012 memoir, *A Natural Woman*. "It was unbelievable how right they were, and we both knew it." Goffin confirmed this in the same chapter, writing, "You made it really easy for me to come out with the lyrics. You made it effortless."

"(You Make Me Feel Like) A Natural Woman" was one of the first singles Franklin released upon signing to Atlantic Records—and it reached No. 8 on the *Billboard* Hot 100, just mere months after she topped the same chart with "Respect." King cut "(You Make Me Feel Like) A Natural Woman" herself on the iconic 1971 LP *Tapestry*, while Mary J. Blige and Celine Dion also covered the song in the 1990s.

Even more notably, Franklin herself honored King by performing a powerful version of the song at the 2015 Kennedy Center Honors—so powerful that then President Barack Obama was overcome with emotion.

AIN'T NO MOUNTAIN HIGH ENOUGH

1967 • MARVIN GAYE AND TAMMI TERRELL

Songwriters: Nickolas Ashford and Valerie Simpson

MUSIC HAS NO shortage of dynamic duos. In the rock realm, there's Paul McCartney and John Lennon, and Mick Jagger and Keith Richards. Country, meanwhile, can claim Tammy Wynette and George Jones *and* Dolly Parton and Porter Wagoner. And in the soul and R&B world, perhaps no duo is bigger than Marvin Gaye and Tammi Terrell. Labelmates on Motown Records, the pair released two collaborative albums and enjoyed a string of hits in the late 1960s—a streak kicked off by "Ain't No Mountain High Enough."

In a nutshell, the song stresses that if someone needs assistance, their beloved will show up and help, no questions asked. No obstacle is too great—not distance, inclement weather, frigid temperatures, a huge river, or (especially) a tall mountain. Gaye and Terrell trade off expressing these sentiments, signifying that the offer of help goes both ways; their voices are urgent but pleasant, underscoring that it's no big deal to be so supportive. The Funk Brothers and the Detroit Symphony Orchestra team up once again to provide brassy, twinkling instrumentation that explodes like a jubilant marching band.

"Ain't No Mountain High Enough" happened to be co-written by another talented duo, Nickolas Ashford and Valerie Simpson, who would later find great success as recording artists using their last names. In 2011, Simpson recalled that Harvey Fuqua and Johnny Bristol—who were producing Gaye and Terrell at the time—asked her and Ashford for potential music. The songwriters parted with "Ain't No Mountain High Enough," a song they had previously held close to their collective vests.

"It's funny because Dusty Springfield had just come to town and wanted to meet with us for material," Simpson told the *Chicago Tribune*. "We played that song for her but wouldn't give it to her because we wanted to hold that back. We felt like that could be our entree to Motown. Nick called it the 'golden egg.'"

Their instincts were right on the mark. "Ain't No Mountain High Enough" reached No. 19 on the *Billboard* Hot 100 but landed at No. 3 on the R&B Singles chart and earned a Grammy nomination for Best Rhythm & Blues Group Performance, Vocal or Instrumental. Although the song lost in this category, it was later inducted into the Grammy Hall of Fame and became a favorite tune heard in multiple movies, including 2014's *Guardians of the Galaxy*. Diana Ross, meanwhile, also covered "Ain't No Mountain High Enough" in 1970. This version hit No. 1 on the *Billboard* Hot 100 and also earned a Grammy nomination for Best Contemporary Vocal Performance (Female).

CAN'T TAKE MY EYES OFF YOU

1967 · FRANKIE VALLI

Songwriters: Bob Crewe and Bob Gaudio

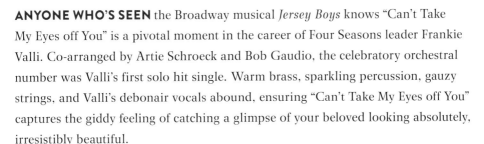

ANYONE WHO'S SEEN the Broadway musical *Jersey Boys* knows "Can't Take My Eyes off You" is a pivotal moment in the career of Four Seasons leader Frankie Valli. Co-arranged by Artie Schroeck and Bob Gaudio, the celebratory orchestral number was Valli's first solo hit single. Warm brass, sparkling percussion, gauzy strings, and Valli's debonair vocals abound, ensuring "Can't Take My Eyes off You" captures the giddy feeling of catching a glimpse of your beloved looking absolutely, irresistibly beautiful.

The song sprang from the pens of Gaudio and Bob Crewe, a duo that had started writing songs together in the early 1960s. Gaudio, who co-wrote the 1958 hit "Short Shorts" while a member of a group called the Royal Teens, was also in the Four Seasons alongside Frankie Valli. Crewe, meanwhile, was later a member of Disco-Tex and the Sex-O-Lettes and co-wrote the LaBelle No. 1 hit "Lady Marmalade" and Valli's chart-topper "My Eyes Adored You."

"Can't Take My Eyes off You" reflected the easy songwriting chemistry between the two men. For example, Crewe provided the song title, Gaudio told Songfacts in 2015. "That was the way we worked: He'd have a list of 20 song titles and if it turned me on, I'd move forward with it, and 'Can't Take My Eyes off You' is one of them." The song's thematic inspiration, however, came from life experience that Gaudio amassed over time. "It's kind of an amalgam of people and circumstances," he said. "Some women, but not one specific, and certain situations that people I've known have found themselves in. You know, I'm pretty observant."

Incredibly enough, Valli told *Parade* in 2014 that "Can't Take My Eyes off You" wasn't released right away. "The record company thought I was looking to leave the group, so they kept it in the can for over a year. I was never leaving. There was another dimension to me that I had to expose to the public to see if it had anything." If anything, the other dimension was simply Valli putting his trademark falsetto to the side and exploring a stronger vocal tone. On the strutting bridge with horns, he positively shouts out his declarations of love, making his true feelings abundantly clear.

When it was finally released, "Can't Take My Eyes off You" took off after the influential Windsor, Ontario, radio station CKLW-AM started playing the song. Getting airplay took some convincing, Gaudio told the *Detroit Free Press* in 2009. Program director Paul Drew only added the tune into rotation after seeing Valli and the Four Seasons perform at a Detroit venue called the Roostertail. "The switchboards lit up and the rest, as they say, is history," Gaudio said.

Indeed, "Can't Take My Eyes off You" reached No. 2 on the *Billboard* Hot 100 in July 1967 and has been covered dozens of times by various artists. Most notably, Ms. Lauryn Hill recorded a hip-hop-influenced version of "Can't Take My Eyes off You" for the 1997 movie *Conspiracy Theory*. Although the tune wasn't on the soundtrack *or* released as a single, the song still became a radio hit after the San Francisco radio station KMEL started playing it. Other stations soon did too, and "Can't Take My Eyes off You" became popular on both pop and R&B radio and was a hidden track on Hill's debut album, *The Miseducation of Lauryn Hill*. For good measure, Hill's version was also nominated for a Grammy Award for Best Female Pop Vocal Performance.

SOMETHING

1969 • THE BEATLES

Songwriter: George Harrison

THE BEATLES WERE no strangers to writing love songs. Early in their career, the Fab Four favored chaste tales of rock 'n' roll puppy love ("I Wanna Hold Your Hand") before eventually branching out into sunny psychedelic pop ("When I'm Sixty-Four") and heart-on-sleeve delicate folk ("I Will").

By the time the 1960s drew to a close, the Beatles started to explore more complex kinds of love songs. Pinned on a lyric said to be taken from the title of an early James Taylor song ("Something in the Way She Moves"), George Harrison's "Something" captures the way attraction grows over time thanks to the features that make someone irresistible. Physical attributes such as a smile or personal aesthetic—or more intangible things like a flirting style or how someone moves—eventually add up to love bolstered by mental and emotional connection.

Harrison started writing "Something" on the piano as the Beatles were finishing up the White Album. "But it was never finished," he said in a September 1969 *Detroit Free Press* interview. "I could never think of the right words for it." He gave the song to Joe Cocker first but had another great artist in mind as it was coming together. "When I recorded it, I imagined someone like Ray Charles doing it, that was the feel I thought it should have," Harrison continued. "But because I'm not Ray Charles—I'm much more limited in what I can do—we just did what we could."

"Something" is certainly no slouch, of course. Along with "Here Comes the Sun"—another Harrison composition—the dewy song is a highlight of *Abbey Road*. The song unfolds on a bed of sinewy guitars and ornate strings that sound like the equivalent of feeling intoxicated by lust and longing. Arrangement-wise, however, it's a marvel: As "Something" moves into a verse that questions the stability of this

Top 10 Love Songs from Movies

1. Bryan Adams, "Everything I Do (I Do It for You)"
(*Robin Hood: Prince of Thieves*)
2. Aerosmith, "I Don't Want to Miss a Thing" (*Armageddon*)
3. Berlin, "Take My Breath Away" (*Top Gun*)
4. Peabo Bryson and Regina Belle, "A Whole New World" (*Aladdin*)
5. Joe Cocker and Jennifer Warnes, "Up Where We Belong"
(*An Officer and a Gentleman*)
6. Glen Hansard and Marketa Irglova, "Falling Slowly" (*Once*)
7. Lady Gaga and Bradley Cooper, "Shallow" (*A Star Is Born*)
8. Bette Midler, "Wind Beneath My Wings" (*Beaches*)
9. Olivia Newton-John, "Hopelessly Devoted to You" (*Grease*)
10. Seal, "Kiss from a Rose" (*Batman Forever*)

attraction, the song becomes louder and more dynamic, employing taut drums from Ringo Starr, lush Hammond organ from Billy Preston, and urgent vocals from Harrison.

In a 2022 interview, Pattie Boyd—who was married to Harrison from 1966 to 1977—recalled that Harrison was actually shy about sharing the tune. "The night before, as all the Beatles were sliding out of Abbey Road, George went to [engineer] Glyn Johns, 'I want to play you a track but I didn't want to do it in front of the others,'" she recalled. "He played 'Something' and Glyn said, 'Are you kidding? That's fabulous. We'll do it tomorrow.'"

Over the years, Harrison could be circumspect about whom he wrote "Something" for, although it's widely considered to be about Boyd. Among other things, he all but confirmed this fact in a 1969 BBC interview, telling the journalist, "Maybe Pattie, probably," when asked who the song was about. In her 2007 autobiography, Boyd herself revealed, "He told me in a matter-of-fact way that he had written it for me. I thought it was beautiful." Fans also adored "Something"—released as a double A-side single with "Come Together," it peaked at No. 1 on the *Billboard* Hot 100 and No. 4 in the UK on the Official Singles chart.

THE FIRST TIME EVER I SAW YOUR FACE

1969 · ROBERTA FLACK

Songwriter: Ewan MacColl

IT'S OFTEN SAID that you only have one chance to make a good first impression. This goes double in matters of love, where a positive first impression can be the difference between romance and heartbreak. Luckily, "The First Time Ever I Saw Your Face" depicts a first meeting that goes spectacularly well—so well that this glimpse leads to a euphoric forever love.

The British folk singer Ewan MacColl wrote "The First Time Ever I Saw Your Face" for Peggy Seeger. The pair first met on March 27, 1956. A video on Seeger's Facebook page notes he was 20 years older—and married with a kid. A snippet of a letter in the video, ostensibly from MacColl, read in part, "I love you, my Peg, and have loved you since I first saw you, and there will never be a time when I don't love

you. We have a lot of living to do together so as to make up for all the time we have lost."

Fittingly, the lyrics of "The First Time Ever I Saw Your Face" are just as poetic. The narrator compares their beautiful face to a sunrise and says their looks brightened up the universe by giving it the moon and the stars—and that's just the first verse! Their first kiss—described as a seismic event on par with an earthquake—leads to a first time being intimate; at that point, the narrator knows their love is eternal.

During the 1960s, artists such as Bonnie Dobson, Gordon Lightfoot, the Kingston Trio, and Peter, Paul and Mary recorded "The First Time Ever I Saw Your Face." But the song rose in stature after Roberta Flack cut a version of the song for her 1969 debut album, *First Take*. With its minimalist instrumentation and leisurely tempo, like a show-stopping cabaret ballad, it teases out the lyrical nuances with palpable sadness, as if she's looking back at a love that's gone away. Unsurprisingly, Flack's inspiration was quite different from that of other artists tackling the song.

"I was thinking about a little black cat that someone had given me, named Sancho Panza," she told Super Seventies RockSite. "I had just gotten back from being on the road for the first time, and I discovered that he had been killed. I only had one pet, and when I went into the studio, two days later, he was still on my mind."

Despite the song's quality, "The First Time Ever I Saw Your Face" wasn't a hit until it appeared in the 1971 Clint Eastwood–directed film *Play Misty for Me*. "The record label wanted to have it re-recorded with a faster tempo," Flack told the Associated Press in 2018, "but Clint said he wanted it exactly as it was." The single spent six weeks atop the *Billboard* Hot 100 in 1972, making it the overall No. 1 song of the year on the Top Pop 100 Singles chart. It also won the Grammy Award for Record of the Year and Song of the Year.

In March 2023, Peggy Seeger remade the song, saying she had started singing the song in January 1957—and stopped performing it in 1989 when MacColl died.

"After that, I had trouble singing it," she wrote. "Then my voice changed and I've hardly sung it at all in the last three decades." Her new version, which she dedicated to Flack, is also permeated with melancholy, courtesy of a gently weathered voice full of wisdom and gravitas.

I'LL BE THERE

1970 • THE JACKSON 5

Songwriters: Hal Davis, Berry Gordy, Willie Hutch, Bob West

BY THE SUMMER of 1970, the Jackson 5 were a certified sensation, thanks to a trio of upbeat, chart-topping tunes: "ABC," "I Want You Back," and "The Love You Save." But for their fourth single, the group decided to slow things down and offer up a midtempo ballad, "I'll Be There." An earnest song with gospel overtones and Beatles-esque instrumentation, it lives up to the title: The tune is a declaration of loyalty and fidelity—through good times and bad, no strings attached. Michael Jackson, who was just 11 years old when he recorded the tune, brings youthful wistfulness to his lead vocal performance, which underscores the song's sincerity.

A formidable songwriting squad wrote "I'll Be There." Berry Gordy founded the legendary Motown, the label to which the Jackson 5 were signed, but he was also a talented songwriter; among the hits he co-wrote included Jackie Wilson's "Lonely Teardrops," the Miracles' "Shop Around," and the Jackson 5's "ABC." The other songwriters also had close Motown ties. Willie Hutch was signed to the label as a recording artist, earning several R&B chart hits while writing songs for other acts on the roster. Hal Davis, meanwhile, also produced "I'll Be There" and later produced Diana Ross's massive hit "Love Hangover." And Bob West was a talented session bassist with dozens of credits to his name.

"I'll Be There" was the Jackson 5's fourth No. 1 single in a row and spent five weeks atop the *Billboard* Hot 100. Despite this previous success, Michael Jackson viewed "I'll Be There" in particular as the group's "real breakthrough song," he wrote in his memoir, *Moon Walk*. "It was the one that said, 'We're here to stay.'"

"I'll Be There" also had massive staying power. Mariah Carey later made the song her own on a 1992 episode of *MTV Unplugged*, transforming it into a plaintive ballad dominated by piano, a gospel choir, and a dynamic featured vocal from the R&B singer Trey Lorenz. This version also reached No. 1 on the *Billboard* Hot 100, spending two weeks at the apex, and was nominated for a Grammy Award for Best R&B Performance by a Duo or Group. Touchingly, Carey and Lorenz also sang the tune at Michael Jackson's 2009 memorial service—bringing a heartbreaking new meaning to the song's pledges of eternal devotion.

MAYBE I'M AMAZED

1970 • PAUL MCCARTNEY

Songwriter: Paul McCartney

THE BEATLES ARE responsible for some of the greatest love songs of all time—to name a few, the raucous ode to teenage love "I Wanna Hold Your Hand," the delicate mash note "In My Life," and the sinewy chronicle of magnetic attraction "Something" (see page 53). When Paul McCartney started the next phase of his career in the 1970s, he doubled down on writing love songs—so much so that his band Wings even released a cheeky tune called "Silly Love Songs" that acknowledged McCartney's fondness for the form.

But few artists penned better love songs than McCartney, as evidenced by "Maybe I'm Amazed," a highlight of his 1970 solo album, *McCartney*. He wrote the song for his beloved wife Linda, whom he married in March 1969. Appropriately enough, inspiration struck as he was playing "the lovely black Steinway piano that we got after our wedding," he wrote in the 2021 book *The Lyrics: 1956 to the Present*. But the song wasn't as straightforward as it might seem on the surface.

"It was to try and get a little deeper into a love song," McCartney told *Billboard* in 2001, calling the song "quirky" and then explaining what he meant. "A straight love song would say, 'I'm amazed at the way you love me.' That would be the Sinatra thing, and it would be called, 'I'm Amazed.' But the 'maybe' is like a guy not quite wanting to admit it."

You can view the hesitation as a natural reaction to being a newlywed—after all, that means there's more at stake if things don't work out—or as McCartney feeling a bit awestruck by the depth of his love *and* his musical chemistry with Linda. But "Maybe I'm Amazed" is also indicative of McCartney's mindset as he wrote the song: The Beatles were in the midst of fracturing, leaving the musician feeling unsteady about his life *and* deeply alone.

Yet Linda banished his insecurities by providing solace, empathy, and support—hence the chorus, during which McCartney shares that a cherished partner is helping him make sense of the world and feel grounded. In a way, "Maybe I'm Amazed" is McCartney confessing his vulnerabilities and fears, even as he acknowledges gratitude for his rock-solid relationship. Or as he put it in *The Lyrics* when discussing "Maybe I'm Amazed," it's based on "the central idea being that there's so often a split between the inner and outer."

McCartney recorded the song in one day, during a February 1970 session in Studio Two at EMI Studios on Abbey Road. He played every instrument himself on "Maybe I'm Amazed"—guitar, bass, piano, and drums—much like he did on the rest of the songs on *McCartney*. In a pointed gesture, however, he and Linda both provided backing vocals; the couple was a "vocal backing group," as he wrote in the 1970 press release for *McCartney*.

"Maybe I'm Amazed" is dominated by pensive and evocative piano distinguished by some bluesy bar-band flourishes but later adds layers of meticulous electric guitars and subtle drums. McCartney's voice becomes more desperate on the chorus, as if to underscore the urgency of his feelings, and sounds ragged in other spots, as if he's overcome by emotion.

Surprisingly, the tune wasn't released as a single, even though it did have a gorgeous music video: a slideshow of intimate Linda McCartney photos that depict the couple's family life. The song became a standard in Wings setlists in the 1970s. A live version immortalized on the 1976 triple live album *Wings Over America* is particularly raw and did become a single; it reached No. 10 on the *Billboard* Hot 100.

Countless artists have covered "Maybe I'm Amazed"—to name a few, the Faces, Billy Joel, Cyndi Lauper and Heart, and Dave Grohl and Norah Jones. The song has also remained a staple of McCartney's setlists over the years and has taken on an even more poignant tone since Linda's 1998 death from breast cancer. Originally written to honor the love McCartney had for her, now it's a moving, tender testament to their long marriage and eternal love.

SIGNED, SEALED, DELIVERED (I'M YOURS)

1970 • STEVIE WONDER

Songwriters: Lee Garrett, Lula Mae Hardaway, Stevie Wonder, Syreeta Wright

THE RAKISH PROTAGONIST of "Signed, Sealed, Delivered (I'm Yours)" knows that he's deeply imperfect. In fact, he'll be the *first* person to admit that he's impulsive and may or may not have stepped out on his partner and then stupidly broken things off. He doesn't excuse this behavior; if anything, he owns up to his mistakes. He's trying to win her back by begging for forgiveness and stating that he's all-in on the relationship.

Produced by Wonder, "Signed, Sealed, Delivered (I'm Yours)" is classic Stevie: note-perfect funk grooves, vivacious horns, soulful backing vocals, and a passionate lead vocal. Wonder penned "Signed, Sealed, Delivered (I'm Yours)" with several other people, including the songwriter and radio DJ Lee Garrett. However, the song was also something of a family affair, as other credited co-writers include Wonder's mom, Lula Mae Hardaway—she apparently came up with the titular phrase—and his soon-to-be wife, the recording artist Syreeta Wright.

Wright and Wonder met when she was working in Motown's arranging department. Their initial attempt at recording a song didn't quite gel—but their romance "blossomed," she said in an interview. That eventually led to a songwriting collaboration on what would turn out to be "Signed, Sealed, Delivered (I'm Yours)." Wright recalled that she "had no experience in lyric-writing" when Wonder asked her to contribute. "All he knew was that I wrote poetry. At first, I thought he was crazy—but since he had confidence in my ability, I wasn't going to say no."

It wasn't the only song they would write together; the couple also teamed up with Garrett for the Spinners' soul hit "It's a Shame." But "Signed, Sealed, Delivered (I'm Yours)" became a massive success, earning two Grammy nominations, topping *Billboard*'s Best Selling Soul Singles chart, and peaking at No. 3 on the Hot 100.

Over the years, the song has been covered dozens of times, including by Peter Frampton, Chaka Khan, Rufus Wainwright, a pre-fame Elton John, and Syreeta Wright herself. Outside of music, "Signed, Sealed, Delivered (I'm Yours)" was a theme song of sorts for Barack Obama's 2008 presidential campaign— and it also became a rollicking group sing-along in the 2021 special *Trolls: Holiday in Harmony.*

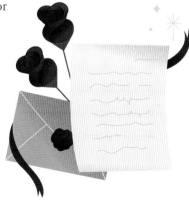

A CASE OF YOU

1971 • JONI MITCHELL

Songwriter: Joni Mitchell

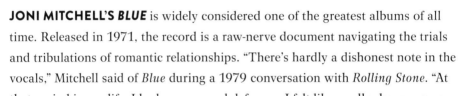

JONI MITCHELL'S *BLUE* is widely considered one of the greatest albums of all time. Released in 1971, the record is a raw-nerve document navigating the trials and tribulations of romantic relationships. "There's hardly a dishonest note in the vocals," Mitchell said of *Blue* during a 1979 conversation with *Rolling Stone*. "At that period in my life, I had no personal defenses. I felt like a cellophane wrapper on a pack of cigarettes. I felt like I had absolutely no secrets from the world and I couldn't pretend in my life to be strong. Or to be happy."

"A Case of You" is one of those brutally honest songs. In the first verse, Mitchell scoffs at a partner who claims (falsely) to be consistent, telling him she's going to the bar instead. While seated, she proceeds to reminisce about their relationship— both the good and the bad—using the metaphor of an intoxicating partnership. But she affirms that no matter how much of him she (figuratively) drinks in, she won't fall; the connotation is that even though things ended badly, she's resilient. The lyrics offer an interesting juxtaposition: A relationship that's sweet and has the potential to disorient you instead leaves you feeling stronger.

The insights are very indicative of Mitchell's approach at the time. Speaking about the songs on *Blue*, she once told the *Los Angeles Times*, "I think men write very dishonestly about breakups. I wanted to be capable of being responsible for my own errors. If there was friction between me and another person, I wanted to be able to see my participation in it so I could see what could be changed and what could not." Musically, however, "A Case of You" is unadorned: Mitchell played Appalachian dulcimer while James Taylor (with whom she famously had a relationship) played guitar.

"A Case of You" has been covered by Tori Amos, k.d. lang, and Prince; the latter renamed it "A Case of U" in his classic alphabet parlance. When Mitchell made her surprise 2022 return to the Newport Folk Festival, "A Case of You" also made the setlist. Brandi Carlile took lead vocals and Mitchell accompanied her, giving particular vocal emphasis to the lines about being steady—a gorgeous duet that amplified the song's ageless message.

LET'S STAY TOGETHER

1972 • AL GREEN

Songwriters: Al Green, Al Jackson Jr., Willie Mitchell

LOVE SONGS DON'T have to be overwrought to be effective. Take Al Green's soul classic "Let's Stay Together," in which the protagonist is very clear about their intentions: They want to be with their chosen one forever—through thick and thin, through ups and downs, and in good *and* bad times. Relationships that are on and off? Green says no way—and he hopes his beloved wouldn't ever break his heart that way.

Green and the song's co-writer and producer, Willie Mitchell, recorded "Let's Stay Together" at Royal Studios in Memphis, Tennessee. (Peppered with an easygoing groove and brassy horn accents, the song *sounds* like a classic Memphis soul tune.) Green reportedly spent five minutes writing the lyrics to "Let's Stay Together," although polishing off the vocals took much longer—eight days, according to Mitchell. "[Green] wouldn't listen to me," he told *the Palm Beach Post.* "He was singing it too hard. I kept telling him, 'Softer, softer!'"

Finally, after Green started to cry—ostensibly out of frustration—the producer found the right words to get the best performance out of him. "I told him, 'You sound like everybody out on the street. I want to hear Al Green.' He told me, 'I don't know who Al Green is.' He left me and went away." Upon returning after some self-reflection, Green finally nailed the song's butter-smooth vocals.

"Let's Stay Together" reached No. 1 on the *Billboard* Hot 100 and the magazine's Best Selling Soul Singles chart and was added to the Library of Congress's National Recording Registry in 2010. Over the years, it's appeared in multiple movies and has been covered dozens of times, including by Shirley Bassey, Boyz II Men, and Al Jarreau. Perhaps the most notable cover is by Tina Turner, whose 1983 version of the song (with co-production by Heaven 17's Martyn Ware) became a top 10 UK hit and helped usher in her comeback as a solo artist.

Several years after the success of "Let's Stay Together," Green was ordained as a minister and started releasing religious music. These beliefs didn't stop him from performing his signature song, however. "Folks are always saying, 'If Al Green was really saved and sanctified, he wouldn't be singing "Let's Stay Together,"'" *the Palm Beach Post* quoted him as saying during a 2003 sermon. "I say, what's wrong with that? What's wrong with singing, 'I want to spend my whole life with you'?"

YOU ARE SO BEAUTIFUL

1974 • JOE COCKER

Songwriters: Bruce Fisher and Billy Preston

A LOVE SONG doesn't have to be elaborate to get its point across. Sometimes the most heartfelt messages are the simplest ones. That's certainly the case with "You Are So Beautiful," which the keyboardist-songwriter Billy Preston wrote for his mother, Robbie Lee Williams, a keyboardist who performed in church. The narrator tells their beloved they are perfect the way they are, repeats the title phrase multiple times, and voilà—that's all the song needs.

Bruce Fisher, who also helped co-write Preston's songs "Will It Go Round in Circles" and "Nothing from Nothing," also collaborated to write "You Are So Beautiful." The version on Preston's 1974 LP *The Kids & Me* very much honors the church roots of Preston's mom, with a sunburst-like choir and strings, as well as an atmosphere that feels rich with salvation.

Joe Cocker inarguably did the most recognizable version of the song. His take is slower and reverent, featuring piano from Nicky Hopkins (of Rolling Stones/Kinks/ the Who fame) and a vocal performance that treats the other person's beauty almost like it's a holy thing. "I did about six passes and the producer, Rob Fraboni, said, 'Give us one more,'" Cocker said in 2010 of his vocals. "Because it was the last one, I did that [*sings broken croak*] 'to me' on the end, the little teardrop sound. And everybody in the control booth lit up." Cocker recorded his version in spring 1974 and it appeared later that year on his LP *I Can Stand a Little Rain*. By March 1975, it had become a major hit, reaching No. 5 on the *Billboard* Hot 100.

But despite the concise elegance of "You Are So Beautiful," the song potentially has a surprisingly complicated history. The Beach Boys' Dennis Wilson also performed his own live version of the song that's even more tender and heartfelt than either of the versions by Cocker or Preston. Incredibly enough, Wilson was rumored to have helped Preston finish the song. According to Jon Stebbins's book *Dennis Wilson: The Real Beach Boy*, Wilson and Preston were at a party, playing piano and hanging with rock royalty such as Three Dog Night's Danny Hutton and America's Gerry Beckley. At some point, "You Are So Beautiful" apparently came up, and Wilson started singing along with Preston—and the tune was allegedly finished that very night.

When asked about it in a 2004 interview, Brian Wilson flatly denied that Dennis wrote the song. Others say he did. "I was there that night," the musician Billy Hinsche said in *Dennis Wilson: The Real Beach Boy*, noting that Dennis Wilson and Preston "really connected" with each other. "And I would not dispute that Dennis had a hand in writing 'You Are So Beautiful,' and that's the reason we would do it in concert." Authorship questions aside, what's not in doubt is the heartfelt message at the core of the song—and how lovely its sentiments remain all these years later.

FOOLED AROUND AND FELL IN LOVE

1975 • ELVIN BISHOP

Songwriter: Elvin Bishop

THERE'S NO RIGHT (or wrong) way to meet a significant other. Sometimes a longtime friendship deepens into a romance; at other times, you'll meet a soulmate through friends or online. And on other occasions still, a romantic encounter that's intended to be a one-night stand unexpectedly turns into something more serious—and permanent.

Elvin Bishop's blues rock–infused "Fooled Around and Fell in Love" describes the latter scenario to a T. At first, the song's protagonist is a grade-A cad who keeps a book of his conquests, has no remorse over ditching a woman if he meets someone better, and doesn't care if his selfish actions cause pain. But one hookup quite suddenly changes his ways: He catches feelings for a woman and finds himself falling head over heels for her.

Despite the raunchy lyrical insinuations and rugged guitars, "Fooled Around and Fell in Love" sounds like an old-fashioned love song. The chorus features starry-eyed harmonies, easygoing piano, and the kind of early rock 'n' roll groove you might hear at a 1950s teen dance. The verses, meanwhile, are dominated by a yearning, soulful lead vocal performance from one of Bishop's backing singers, Mickey Thomas. Thomas brings humanity and sensitivity to his delivery—making the protagonist seem like a sympathetic figure, not a creep or a chauvinist.

Bishop started off as a guitarist in the Paul Butterfield Blues Band before forming the Elvin Bishop Group. By the mid-1970s, however, he started releasing albums under his own name. Enter *Struttin' My Stuff*, the 1975 LP that featured "Fooled Around and Fell in Love." In a Songfacts interview about songwriting, Bishop said, "The better a song is, the less story there is to it, as far as I can tell. The best songs just come rushing out." Accordingly, "Fooled Around and Fell in Love" was one of those tunes. He added: "That song just damn near wrote itself."

When it came time to record "Fooled Around and Fell in Love," Bishop cut a version himself but wasn't thrilled with the results—"I said, 'That's not buttering my biscuit, my vocal on this,'" Bishop told Songfacts—and suggested Thomas might be better suited for the job. "He can sing a page out of the phone book and move people," Bishop said. "And my voice is very plain. It's better suited for blues."

Thomas indeed was the right person to handle the vocals. In fact, this performance raised his profile considerably, and by the end of the 1970s, he had joined Jefferson Starship. Bishop also enjoyed massive success, landing his biggest hit ever with "Fooled Around and Fell in Love," which peaked at No. 3 on the *Billboard* Hot 100.

"Fooled Around and Fell in Love" has been a favorite song for country artists to cover. T. G. Sheppard had a hit with the tune in 1985, while in 2019, Miranda Lambert cut the song with the artists who opened her Roadside Bars & Pink Guitars Tour. The celebratory collaborative version of "Fooled Around and Fell in Love"—which ended up featuring Maren Morris, Ashley McBryde, Tenille Townes, Elle King, and Caylee Hammack—won the ACM Award for Vocal Event of the Year.

LOVE WILL KEEP US TOGETHER

1975 • CAPTAIN & TENNILLE

Songwriters: Howard Greenfield and Neil Sedaka

ON A PRAGMATIC level, romantic couples decide to stay together for many reasons: convenience, children, finances, and even laziness. In a perfect world, however, the glue that keeps most people together is *love*. That's the obvious premise of "Love Will Keep Us Together," a 1975 pop song popularized by Captain & Tennille, the husband-wife duo of Daryl "Captain" Dragon and Toni Tennille.

Over and over again, the song's narrator aims to reassure their partner that they'll always be faithful and true. The couple is on rock-solid ground because of their love; any extramarital flirtations or romantic fakes are mere distractions. Buoyed by this earnest tone, "Love Will Keep Us Together" pairs Dragon's bouncy keyboards and light funk grooves with Hal Blaine's steady drumming flourishes. Tennille is the real star of the song, however, belting out the lyrics with confidence and sass—making it abundantly clear where she stands on fidelity.

Beneath the enthusiastic surface, however, "Love Will Keep Us Together" certainly has some pointed lyrics. For example, the narrator says they'll continue to love their partner forever—even when their partner's youthful beauty fades and other people are no longer attracted to them. At other points, the narrator warns their partner not to lose focus if other people come around and try to flirt with them. That Tennille issues these warnings offers an interesting perspective flip, as you might expect a man to exhibit such casual sexism instead.

Thematically, "Love Will Keep Us Together" grew out of an agonizing scenario: a schism between Neil Sedaka and his longtime writing partner Howard Greenfield.

The pair co-wrote 1971's *Emergence*, a lush, symphonic LP about which Sedaka was excited. Unfortunately, the album wasn't a success, which "shattered Howie Greenfield and me," Sedaka told Songfacts. "We split up for two-and-a-half years. It was very sad. [Greenfield] moved to California."

Before parting ways, the duo came together to write "Love Will Keep Us Together," which Sedaka thought "was kind of like his plea. We both cried after we wrote it." Musically, however, Sedaka was inspired by more upbeat things while writing the song: Diana Ross's inimitable voice, the swinging groove of the Beach Boys' song "Do It Again," and the augmented chords favored by Al Green.

Sedaka cut "Love Will Keep Us Together" first, and it appeared on 1974's *Sedaka's Back* LP. Captain & Tennille ended up recording the song after Kip Cohen, a producer from A&M Records, played them Sedaka's version. "And Toni Tennille fell off her chair," Sedaka told Paul Shaffer during a 2020 SiriusXM interview. "She said, 'We're going in tomorrow [to] record that song.'" As it turned out, Captain & Tennille needed another song to record for their debut album.

Captain & Tennille's "Love Will Keep Us Together" spent four weeks at No. 1 on the *Billboard* Hot 100 and ended up as the overall top song of 1975. For good measure, the song also took home a Grammy Award for Record of the Year. Captain & Tennille cut a Spanish version of the song ("Por Amor Viviremos") that also reached the *Billboard* Hot 100 and later rerecorded "Love Will Keep Us Together" for a 1995 album called *Twenty Years of Romance*.

Paradoxically, however, the song's promise of fealty and longevity didn't extend to the duo's relationship. Years later, the couple went through a high-profile (and occasionally acrimonious) divorce. Sedaka kept things lighter, recording a version called "Lunch Will Keep Us Together" in 2009 for his children's album, *Waking Up Is Hard to Do*.

LOVIN' YOU

1975 • MINNIE RIPERTON

Songwriters: Minnie Riperton and Richard Rudolph

LOVE SONGS DON'T need to be complicated to be effective. In fact, sometimes the most romantic tunes use unadorned language to express love and affection. That's certainly the case with Minnie Riperton's languid soul-folk classic "Lovin' You," which overflows with effusive—but straightforward—compliments.

Throughout "Lovin' You," the narrator compares life with their partner to springtime—a lovely image, since it's the season of rebirth and new beginnings— and praises their partner's beautiful soul and colorful essence. It's clear that their relationship is an idyllic one full of enviable romantic bliss. In fact, the song only becomes cryptic when it hints that the couple's love becomes richer in the bedroom. Riperton enhances this vibe with a honey-sweet performance touched with tender desperation and her trademark high-register, sighing trills.

Riperton—who was part of the psychedelic Chicago band Rotary Connection before going solo—co-wrote "Lovin' You" with her husband, Richard Rudolph. Despite its overt romantic vibe, it ended up being a lullaby for the couple's daughter, the actress and musician Maya Rudolph. (On the album version of the song, Riperton even gently sings "Maya" over and over again to close the song.) But Rudolph actually started writing "Lovin' You" in 1971, before Maya was even born.

"After Maya was born, I'd play the song all the time at the little house we had in Gainesville," he told *Mix*, recalling that the "idyllic" property boasted things like a duck pond and a hammock. "One day while Minnie was cooking, she started to hum along, and she came up with the final melody. Then I wrote the lyrics and developed the bridge."

The couple made a sparse demo of the song featuring Riperton singing to guitar accompaniment. A loop of this music, which they played for young Maya, pulled double duty for the couple, Rudolph admitted: "It would make her think her mother was there while Minnie and I slipped off for some private time!" This Gainesville demo would also eventually come into play as they were recording Riperton's 1974 album, *Perfect Angel*.

Stevie Wonder, using the pseudonym "El Toro Negro," was co-producing alongside Rudolph at the Record Plant. Getting the right recording was proving challenging, so the studio crew used this demo as a guide, with Rudolph adding warm guitar and Wonder contributing burbling Fender Rhodes (an electric keyboard). To add the perfect touch of natural ambiance, they went to the UCLA botanical garden, where Riperton crooned with a bird; these tranquil tweeting sounds appear throughout, adding whimsy.

"Lovin' You" spent one week at No. 1 on the *Billboard* Hot 100 in 1975. And while Riperton released four subsequent albums, she died of breast cancer in 1979, preventing her from seeing "Lovin' You" and *Perfect Angel* take their rightful place as classics.

HOW DEEP IS YOUR LOVE

1977 • BEE GEES

Songwriters: Barry Gibb, Maurice Gibb, Robin Gibb

HOW DEEP IS your love? It's an age-old query that doubles as a fidelity test. That's certainly clear from the Bee Gees song of the same name: The narrator is repeatedly asking this question because their crush keeps teasing them with affection before leaving once again.

At heart, however, "How Deep Is Your Love" is a song about longing—and reassuring someone else that they're the right person for you. Take the chorus: Even if the world might be trying to conspire against the relationship, the lyrics crest with an empathetic sentiment of solidarity. In the end, the couple can weather the storm together.

This vibe was no accident, Robin Gibb said in the 2011 book *The Bee Gees: Tales of The Brothers Gibb*. "Personalities are examined in that tune, but female or male aren't even mentioned in it. It has universal connotations and it clicks with everyone." That universality made "How Deep Is Your Love" ideal for inclusion in a movie soundtrack. Luckily, the producer Robert Stigwood had reached out to the Bee Gees to see if they had some songs for a movie he was making—a film that ended up being the 1977 disco-era smash *Saturday Night Fever*. As it so happens, the Bee Gees did have a batch earmarked for an album of their own, including "How Deep Is Your Love," "Stayin' Alive," and "More Than a Woman."

As Barry Gibb recalled in a 1989 interview (cited in *The Bee Gees: Tales of The Brothers Gibb*), they recorded these songs in a television-free French chateau "in really bad weather, with nothing else to do." This was the perfect environment for songwriting, he added. "There was no other form of entertainment, so you literally had to go to work. We couldn't be lazy." In fact, they mixed "How Deep Is Your Love" six times.

In the same book, co-producer Albhy Galuten noted that keyboardist Blue Weaver also "had a tremendous amount of input," in the song, including "a lot of influence in the piano structure of that song." Weaver elaborated on what this meant, describing a very early morning session where he and Barry Gibb worked up a demo together in the studio.

"What happened was, I'd throw chords at him and he'd say, 'No, not that chord,' and I'd keep moving around and he'd say, 'Yeah, that's a nice one' and we'd go from there," Weaver said. "Then I'd play another thing—sometimes, I'd be following the melody line that he already had and sometimes I'd most probably lead him somewhere else by doing what I did." The group subsequently finished "How Deep Is Your Love" at Criteria Studios in Miami, adding electric piano. The results

Top 10 Songs About Bad Partners

1. Phoebe Bridgers, "Motion Sickness"
2. The Cranberries, "Linger"
3. Destiny's Child, "Say My Name"
4. Ms. Lauryn Hill, "(Doo Wop) That Thing"
5. Lady Gaga, "Bad Romance"
6. Katy Perry, "Hot N Cold"
7. Pink, "Just Like a Pill"
8. Rihanna, "Love the Way You Lie"
9. Britney Spears, "Toxic"
10. The Supremes, "Baby Love"

are lush and classic. The Gibbs' angelic familial harmonies flow like a tranquil stream above a sterling R&B groove dotted with strings.

"How Deep Is Your Love" was the group's first hit from the blockbuster *Saturday Night Fever* soundtrack and spent three weeks atop the *Billboard* Hot 100. The song also won a Grammy Award for Best Pop Performance by a Group and was also nominated for a Golden Globe.

In later years, Take That did a version of the song, while NSYNC covered "How Deep Is Your Love" as part of a live Bee Gees medley, including once with Barry Gibb at the 2003 Grammy Awards. Gibb also later rerecorded the song on his 2021 album, *Greenfields: The Gibb Brothers Songbook, Vol. 1.*

JUST THE WAY YOU ARE

1977 · BILLY JOEL

Songwriter: Billy Joel

ONE OF THE most loving gifts a partner can give you is acceptance. In fact, being told that you're perfect as is—that you don't need to change a thing about yourself to be loved—is incredibly powerful. That's the premise of Billy Joel's '70s soft rock smash "Just the Way You Are," which appeared on his fifth album, *The Stranger.* Joel stresses that his partner doesn't need to change her style or look or try and impress him with fancy conversation. Instead, he simply accepts and adores her for who she is—that's all he needs *and* wants.

In a 2010 Howard Stern interview, Joel noted that song title inspiration came from a line in the Frankie Valli and the Four Seasons song "Rag Doll"—a tune that also inspired Joel's 1983 megahit "Uptown Girl." But "Just the Way You Are" was more intentionally written for Joel's then wife, Elizabeth Weber, to whom he was married from 1973 to 1982. Although Joel subsequently remarried (and divorced) several times, he didn't play "Just the Way You Are" for many years because it was about Weber. "I've still got a lot of sourness about that," he told *the Atlanta Journal-Constitution* in 1994.

In a nod to its happier origins, "Just the Way You Are" possesses a warm tone, courtesy of Joel playing an introspective Fender Rhodes. Vocally, he and producer Phil Ramone were inspired by an equally enveloping song from the UK rock band 10cc—ostensibly "I'm Not in Love"—for Joel's prominent overdubbed backing vocals.

"We tried an unusual overlapping of his voice, so eventually we could actually play the samples," Ramone said in an interview, describing how the harmonies came together in the studio. "Each note of the scale—the root, the third, the fifth, and the octave. That put us in a place where when you turned this up, because it was recorded, I could give it this very eerie [vibe]." A meditative solo from the noted jazz alto saxophonist Phil Woods rounded out the sentimental mood.

In a 2008 interview, Joel said they almost didn't include "Just the Way You Are" on *The Stranger* "because we really didn't like it that much," but were persuaded to put it on the LP by two major 1970s artists, Phoebe Snow and Linda Ronstadt. "They said, 'You guys are crazy, you've gotta keep that on the album,'" Joel said. "We said 'Yeah? Well, okay, I guess girls like that song, it's a chick song.'"

"Just the Way You Are" became Billy Joel's first US top 10 hit, peaking at No. 3, and topped *Billboard*'s Easy Listening chart. The song also won two of the biggest Grammy Awards: Record of the Year and Song of the Year. He's also warmed up to the song again, setting aside any unpleasant connotations in favor of putting it back into live rotation.

ESCAPE (THE PIÑA COLADA SONG)

1979 • RUPERT HOLMES

Songwriter: Rupert Holmes

QUITE UNDERSTANDABLY, CHEATING is often a relationship dealbreaker—not least because it's a serious breach of trust. But with the breezy "Escape (The Piña Colada Song)," Rupert Holmes crafted one of the few songs where cheating actually *saves* a relationship.

With an easygoing groove that resembles a swaying palm tree and flourishes like beachy guitars, "Escape (The Piña Colada Song)" is more like an intrigue-filled short story. A man decides that he's tired of his boring long-term relationship and finds a promising personal ad: a smart woman looking for a man who hates yoga but enjoys tropical drinks, rain showers, and late-night lovemaking. Excited, he responds, saying he digs her vibe, enjoys champagne, and isn't into health food—and suggests meeting the very next day at a bar. When he shows up, who should walk in? His lady. Instead of being angry, she marvels at the coincidence—and the couple recommit to putting more adventure into their relationship.

Like a good piece of fiction, "Escape (The Piña Colada Song)" requires some willing suspension of disbelief; after all, the man justifies his affair by saying his boredom trumped any empathy for his partner. (*She* doesn't know that, of course, which introduces another wrinkle of deception.) And like many novellas, the song also came together over an extended period of time that was full of twists and turns.

In an interview with ClassicBands.com, Holmes noted "Escape (The Piña Colada Song)" grew out of a complicated tune called "People Need Other People," which he had earmarked for his fifth LP, *Partners in Crime*. Unfortunately, the recording session was tumultuous—among other things, a drummer fell unconscious after only one take of the song, which necessitated some savvy editing to salvage 16 bars of usable music—and Holmes needed to come up with an entirely new song, including lyrics.

Up against a deadline, he mined vibrant source material for the song, letting his imagination run wild upon perusing the personal ad section of the *Village Voice*. "The next day, I took a taxi into the session," he told ClassicBands.com. "I read the lyric to the cab driver and asked him if he guessed the ending before I got to it. He said 'No,' and he liked the story." At the studio, Holmes sang the song through once and planned on redoing his vocals later—but eventually concluded that the charismatic first take was best.

During this whirlwind, Holmes also made one other important change to "Escape (The Piña Colada Song)." Initially, he was going to mention actor Humphrey Bogart in the song's lyrics but told *Hudson Valley* magazine he changed his mind at the last minute because he "thought that reference was too noir."

Instead, Holmes swapped in the reference to the decadent cocktail—which, ironically enough, he swore he had never drunk before. "I wanted something that makes you think of the tropics," he said, "because when you go on an escape vacation, the first day you're on the beach you never order a Budweiser, because you want to announce to yourself and to the world that you are officially on a vacation, an escape."

"Escape (The Piña Colada Song)" spent three nonconsecutive weeks at No. 1 on the *Billboard* Hot 100 and has had an incredible afterlife, appearing in movies like *Guardians of the Galaxy* and *Grown Ups*, and in TV commercials for Taco Bell and *Bachelor in Paradise*.

CRAZY LITTLE THING CALLED LOVE

1979 • QUEEN

Songwriter: Freddie Mercury

IN THE LATE 1970s and early 1980s, the blazing rock 'n' roll style of rockabilly had a resurgence. Although restless punk rockers naturally gravitated toward the raucous genre—notably ex–Tuff Darts vocalist Robert Gordon and Los Angeles group the Blasters—rockabilly also came overground in groups like the Brian Setzer–led new wave fave Stray Cats.

Ever scholars of music history, the UK rock band Queen also dipped their toes into a swinging rockabilly groove on "Crazy Little Thing Called Love." The narrator is a cool-as-a-cucumber, unflappable biker who is *completely shook up* by falling in love with someone spectacular. Metaphorically, the song's lyrics compare the experience to a crying baby, a quivering jellyfish, and swing and jive dances. As the song progresses, our narrator tries to prepare mentally for the romance, mainly by hitting the road for a long motorcycle trip. Playing it cool is difficult, however; love is just too delightfully disorienting.

Mercury wrote "Crazy Little Thing Called Love" in Munich, Germany, while "in the bath in the Bayerischer Hof Hotel," according to drummer Roger Taylor. Incredibly enough, the song came together in "five or ten minutes," Mercury told *Melody Maker*. "I did that on the guitar, which I can't play for nuts."

If it seemed strange that he would choose an instrument he didn't know well—especially when his Queen bandmate Brian May was considered one of the best rock guitarists around—Mercury didn't see it that way. "It's a good discipline because I simply had to write within a small framework," he continued. "I couldn't work through too many chords and because of that restriction I wrote a good song, I think."

May wasn't offended—in an interview with Absolute Radio, he said "Crazy Little Thing Called Love" was almost done by the time he reached the studio—and he even praised the song as Mercury's tribute to the UK star Cliff Richard and the king of rock 'n' roll himself, Elvis Presley. The latter is a particularly obvious influence, between the swinging guitar riffs, walking bass line, lush, Jordanaires-esque backing harmonies, and brushed drums. Mercury even does his best Presley vocal impression, unleashing some hunka-hunka-burning love flourishes in his lower register. "It does sound very authentic," May said of the song's vibe. "Everything about it is sort of like original rock 'n' roll–sounding."

"Crazy Little Thing Called Love" reached No. 2 in the UK but became Queen's first No. 1 single in the US; it spent four weeks atop the *Billboard* Hot 100 in early 1980. Upon the release of the 2018 Freddie Mercury biopic, *Bohemian Rhapsody*, the song surfaced in the top 20 on *Billboard*'s Hot Rock songs chart alongside multiple other Queen hits. And in the spirit of rockabilly's penchant for producing standards, other artists have covered "Crazy Little Thing Called Love." Most notably, country star Dwight Yoakam had a No. 1 hit in Canada with a twanging 1999 take on the song.

YOU MAKE MY DREAMS

1980 · DARYL HALL AND JOHN OATES

Songwriters: Sara Allen, Daryl Hall, John Oates

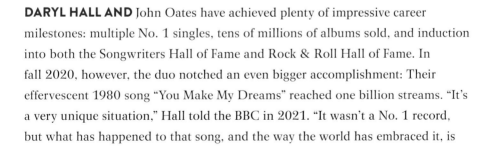

DARYL HALL AND John Oates have achieved plenty of impressive career milestones: multiple No. 1 singles, tens of millions of albums sold, and induction into both the Songwriters Hall of Fame and Rock & Roll Hall of Fame. In fall 2020, however, the duo notched an even bigger accomplishment: Their effervescent 1980 song "You Make My Dreams" reached one billion streams. "It's a very unique situation," Hall told the BBC in 2021. "It wasn't a No. 1 record, but what has happened to that song, and the way the world has embraced it, is absolutely astounding."

It's easy to see why "You Make My Dreams"—which indeed only reached No. 5 on the US *Billboard* Hot 100 and wasn't even a single in the UK at all—connected in a big way with modern audiences. A bouncy collision between synthesizers and guitars that was garnished by bubbly R&B/soul harmonies, "You Make My Dreams" might be the quintessential Daryl Hall and John Oates song. As Oates himself told Songfacts, the tune "represents a vibe" and "a collaboration between myself and Daryl and the band in the studio in the '80s . . . Its simplicity and directness is [sic] where the charm lies in that song."

Accordingly, "You Make My Dreams" came about initially as the result of a spontaneous dressing room jam session between Oates and a guitarist pal. "I started playing a Delta blues, and he started playing a Texas swing," he told Songfacts, "and we put them together, and all of a sudden into my head popped 'you make my dreams.' I just started singing it . . . And it sounded really cool and everyone liked it." Hall remembered things a little differently, telling the BBC: "There's other names on the credits, but I pretty much wrote the song. I was by myself, I started playing that riff on a piano and it just felt good to me, so I started writing the song."

The lyrics continue this ecstatic vibe, speaking to how good it feels when you find someone who completes you—in other words, when you meet your dream partner. Metaphorically, the song contains some evocative imagery: how a candle and its flame feed off each other, for example, or how a partner helps you organize chaotic thoughts. That last reference might have something to do with the song's co-writer: Sara Allen, Hall's partner at the time. "She was really good at jumping into my thoughts and helping me to sort of coalesce them," Hall told Songfacts, when asked about having his girlfriend as a writing collaborator. "That's really what it was all about."

Still, Oates told the BBC that not everybody recognized the song's appeal. "When we played the demo to our manager, his reaction was: 'Who the hell do you guys think you are, Wordsworth?'" Plenty of people did find poetry in the song's words, however. "You Make My Dreams" appeared prominently in two romantic films—Adam Sandler's '80s-inspired comedy, *The Wedding Singer*, and as the song soundtracking an impromptu street shimmy during the indie favorite *(500) Days of Summer*. It was also used to comedic effect in 2008's *Step Brothers* starring Will Ferrell and John C. Reilly.

JUST THE TWO OF US

1980 · GROVER WASHINGTON JR. FEATURING BILL WITHERS

Songwriters: Ralph MacDonald, William Salter, Bill Withers

GROVER WASHINGTON JR.'S "Just the Two of Us" is just as its name implies: an ode to the idea that a relationship is stronger when two people are in sync *and* in love. In fact, the couple is more powerful—and can achieve bigger things—because they're together. They don't need anybody else but each other.

"Just the Two of Us" emerged as Washington—a jazz saxophonist who experienced crossover pop and soul success in the 1970s—was making a new record called *Winelight* alongside a collaborator named Ralph MacDonald, who had also co-written the Roberta Flack and Donny Hathaway hit "Where Is the Love." But "Just the Two of Us" wasn't quite working as an instrumental.

Enter Bill Withers, who possessed one of the smoothest and most expressive soul voices around, as evidenced by R&B hits like "Ain't No Sunshine" and "Lovely Day." "Ralph [MacDonald] called up one day and said, 'We've got this song on Grover's album and it doesn't quite work with the saxophone. Would you sing the song?'" Withers said during a 1981 appearance on *The Merv Griffin Show.* "So I said, 'Send it out, and if I like it then I'll sing it.'"

Withers indeed liked the tune, which was then a sparkling fusion of low-lit R&B and mellow jazz. In addition to Washington on sizzling saxophone, "Just the Two of Us" featured contributions from legendary session musicians—including drummer Steve Gadd and Richard Tee on electric piano—as well as steel drums from Trinidadian musician Robert Greenidge.

But Withers had his own ideas about the words. "I wanted to change some of the lyrics because it was such a soft song," he told Griffin, adding, "I'm an incurable romantic anyway." In a later interview with Songfacts, Withers noted he "probably threw in the stuff like the crystal raindrops, as opposed to what it used to be," and that the "just the two of us" concept already existed. "It was trying to put a tuxedo on it. I didn't like what was said leading up to 'just the two of us.'"

MacDonald's 2011 *Billboard* obituary provided an additional dimension to the song, noting that "Just the Two of Us" is "actually MacDonald's ode to his parents' birthplace, Trinidad and Tobago, whose indigenous calypso and steel pan music provided a source of profound inspiration throughout his illustrious career."

At any rate, Withers knew exactly how to make "Just the Two of Us" a success, adding open-hearted vocals that were both affectionate and confident. "They already had the music recorded, so I just had to go back there and sing," he said. "It didn't seem like work. You know, you can slave over records and you put in everything and [spend] hours in the studio and you spend all kinds of money and you get crazy and sometimes nothing happens. But this was a fun thing because it was just easy and it was very nice."

"Just the Two of Us" peaked at No. 2 on the *Billboard* Hot 100 and won a Grammy Award for Best R&B Song on the way to becoming a signature song for both Washington and Withers. The tune also became an indelible part of pop culture through a few different channels, including being sampled by Eminem on "'97 Bonnie & Clyde" and sung by Dr. Evil in the movie *Austin Powers: The Spy Who Shagged Me*. And in 1997, Will Smith used the original Washington song as the basis for his own single called "Just the Two of Us" that transformed the tune into one lovingly honoring the bond between a father and son.

DON'T STOP BELIEVIN'

1981 · JOURNEY

Songwriters: Jonathan Cain, Steve Perry, Neal Schon

IT WAS THE song heard 'round the world. During the June 10, 2007, finale of beloved TV show *The Sopranos*, Journey's "Don't Stop Believin'" starts playing softly in the background of a diner as Tony (James Gandolfini) eats with his wife, Carmela (Edie Falco), and son A.J. (Robert Iler). The song's rippling piano chords and jagged guitar riffs swell as vocalist Steve Perry, sounding as if he's in a pulpit delivering a solemn benediction, sings about lonely people finding each other in an improbable place.

"Don't Stop Believin'" wasn't exactly obscure before *The Sopranos*; the song reached No. 9 on the *Billboard* Hot 100 back in 1981. But the high-profile appearance made the song into a phenomenon—and reintroduced it into pop culture as a testament to the power of optimism and resilience, particularly in love.

"Don't Stop Believin'" starts by describing a very relatable occurrence: a chance meeting that turns into a passionate night out. The subjects are a girl and boy from opposite places—she's from a small town, he's from the city—who happen to be on the same late-night train. The pair cross paths at a club and connect over a shared smile, leading to their dalliance. This romantic success is held up as an example of keeping

the faith that love can be around any corner—and often happens when you least expect it.

Of course, this fact isn't always obvious from the lyrics, which can be obtuse or head-scratching; for example, there's a reference to a place called South Detroit, which doesn't exist. Perry later explained that the line came from a highway exit sign he saw with the two words.

Journey keyboardist Jonathan Cain told the *Spokesman-Review* the song title also has roots in career advice he received from his dad: "'Don't stop believin', Jon.'" Cain added that he wrote this down in a notebook, which came in handy when Perry needed some lyric ideas: "The clock was ticking on us and Steve wanted to know if there was anything in my magic notebook. I shared with him the phrase 'Don't stop believin'.'"

A real-life experience in Detroit after a Journey show inspired the most evocative part of Perry's lyrics, which reinforce the hope-springs-eternal approach to a night out looking for love. "The streetlights in Detroit at the time were this kind of orange color," he told the Library of Congress in 2022, upon the occasion of the song being added to the prestigious National Recording Registry. "It's like three in the morning and these people were still standing around, and I thought, 'Wow, look at these streetlight people, they're just out in the night.'"

The appearance on *The Sopranos* was just the start of the "Don't Stop Believin'" revival. A 2009 cover by the cast of *Glee* became a surprise global hit, reaching No. 4 in the US and No. 2 in the UK. A 2020 spoof by the comedy duo LadBaby called "Don't Stop Me Eatin'" became the coveted Christmas No. 1 single in the UK. And in Ireland—where both Journey's take and the *Glee* cover reached the singles chart top 5—the song is massive. Today, "Don't Stop Believin'" is also a popular song to play as events are ending—a little note of optimism, perhaps, to keep hope alive as people scatter into the night.

ENDLESS LOVE

1981 • LIONEL RICHIE AND DIANA ROSS

Songwriter: Lionel Richie

LIONEL RICHIE IS no stranger to soundtracking romantic moments. After all, he spent the 1970s as a member of the Commodores, a troupe known for love-soaked songs such as "Three Times a Lady" and "Sweet Love." But his Diana Ross duet "Endless Love"—the title song of *Endless Love*, a 1981 Brooke Shields movie notable for being Tom Cruise's first film—is especially poignant.

The song resembles the vows of fidelity made by a newly married couple who are completely, utterly besotted with each other. Richie and Ross trade off pledging heartfelt declarations of unity, referencing things like two hearts beating as one and shared breathing. With melodramatic, orchestrated accompaniment augmented by big names—including Little Feat guitarist Fred Tackett and session greats like guitarist Paul Jackson Jr. and bassist Nathan East—"Endless Love" unfurls like a graceful, choreographed dance.

So how did "Endless Love" come about? First, *Endless Love* director Franco Zeffirelli asked Richie to submit a song for the soundtrack. At the suggestion of country star Kenny Rogers, with whom Lionel was working at the time, Richie sent in a very rough instrumental sketch of two verses. Zeffirelli was impressed. "Other famous musical composers had submitted complete tapes—the strings, the horns and the lyrics," Richie told *the Minneapolis Star*. "But he said, 'I want that bah-bah song. Lionel, you go home and finish the bah-bah song.'"

On a time crunch to write lyrics, Richie holed up for two hours in the place where he was most inspired: the bathroom in his Beverly Hills house. His eventual vocal recording session with Ross was just as compressed. The pair met in a Reno,

Nevada, studio *after* Ross played a show in Lake Tahoe and knocked out their parts in a three-hour stretch that ended at 6 a.m.

"Endless Love" spent a whopping nine weeks at No. 1 on the *Billboard* Hot 100 in 1981 and ended up at No. 2 on the magazine's year-end pop singles list. Impressively, the song also topped *Billboard*'s Adult Contemporary and R&B charts in 1981, paving the way for "Endless Love" to win two trophies at the American Music Awards, in the pop/rock and soul singles categories. For good measure, Richie was also nominated for Best Original Song at the Academy Awards for "Endless Love," while Ross recorded a solo version for her 1981 album, *Why Do Fools Fall in Love.*

Fittingly, "Endless Love" has had a rather, well, endless long tail. Luther Vandross later recorded a gorgeous cover of the song with Mariah Carey. This version also became a success; in fact, it was Vandross's biggest crossover hit ever, reaching No. 2 on the *Billboard* Hot 100. Years later, Richie returned to the adult contemporary charts with a new duet version of "Endless Love" recorded with country music singer Shania Twain for his 2012 country album, *Tuskegee.*

SEXUAL HEALING

1982 • MARVIN GAYE

Songwriters: Odell Brown, Marvin Gaye, David Ritz

SOME LOVE SONGS are romantic; some are meant to be sentimental; still others function as foreplay. And then there's Marvin Gaye's "Sexual Healing," a luxurious R&B seduction that's rightfully held up as a paragon of come-hither baby-making music. Atop a silky groove and Gaye's pleasure-seeking croon, the tune makes no secret of its burning desire for sexual satisfaction—in person, on the phone, in

Top 10 Breakup Songs

1. Cher, "Believe"

2. Destiny's Child, "Survivor"

3. Fleetwood Mac, "Go Your Own Way"

4. Gloria Gaynor, "I Will Survive"

5. Ariana Grande, "thank u, next"

6. No Doubt, "Don't Speak"

7. Sinéad O'Connor, "Nothing Compares 2 U"

8. Taylor Swift, "We Are Never Ever Getting Back Together"

9. Usher, "Burn"

10. Amy Winehouse, "Back to Black"

the morning, at night, *whenever*. What matters is that the narrator is in lust and positively *craving* his partner's body and soul. For good measure, Gaye emphasizes this urgency—and his sexual appetite—by occasionally rising into falsetto or sliding into a whisper.

"Sexual Healing" was co-written by David Ritz, who eventually penned Gaye's biography *Divided Soul: The Life of Marvin Gaye*. Ritz told SongwriterUniverse that Gaye was initially "obsessed with" a "reggae-styled rhythm track" from keyboardist and co-writer Odell Brown as the song's foundation. Other accounts of the song's recording mention Gaye piling on guitar tracks, as well as new technology like a TR-808 drum machine and Jupiter-8 synthesizer. The latter two instruments gave the song a unique percolating, percussion-bubbled groove.

"As far as I know, he was the first person to program a TR-808 as its own instrument instead of trying to imitate a drum kit," engineer Mike Butcher told

Electronic Sound. "He would do things like put the side-stick on a beat, which a drummer wouldn't do." In the documentary *808*, Butcher added there was a good reason Gaye turned to these instruments: "He wanted to use synthesizers and drum machines so he could do it all himself. He didn't want anyone else involved."

But Gaye needed lyrics—and Ritz explained to SongwriterUniverse he had just the idea, based around what the tune *shouldn't* be: reminiscent of an "avant-garde, French sadomasochistic book" Gaye had on his coffee table. "I told Marvin, 'This is sick. What you need is sexual healing, being in love with one woman, where sex and love are joined instead of sexual perversity.'"

The idea of "sexual healing" appealed to Gaye, Ritz added, and the men set to work crafting a song. "I wrote most of the lyrics, including all of the verses and the chorus lyric, and Marvin wrote the melody and the bridge lyric," said Ritz. "I wrote the lyrics like a poem, and the entire lyric was finished in about 30 minutes." Gaye was thrilled, he added. "Marvin immediately loved the song, and he thought it would be a hit. He said, 'This is what I've been looking for.'"

"Sexual Healing" indeed did function as a major catalyst for Gaye's early 1980s comeback—a resurgence that came after a challenging period that found him splitting from his second wife, navigating tax issues, and overcoming mental health challenges and substance misuse. Released on 1982's *Midnight Love*, the single peaked at No. 3 on the *Billboard* Hot 100 and topped the Black Singles chart on the way to winning a Grammy Award for Best Male R&B Vocal Performance. Sadly, however, "Sexual Healing" was Gaye's last top 10 hit, as the singer died in 1984.

ALWAYS ON MY MIND

1982 · WILLIE NELSON

Songwriters: Wayne Carson Thompson, Johnny Christopher, Mark James

"ALWAYS ON MY MIND" is based on a very simple premise: Even if you're in a loving relationship, chances are good that at some point you'll hurt your partner's feelings and need to apologize. Figuring out *how* to respond when you're in this situation makes all the difference. The song suggests that it's best to acknowledge your mistakes and share exactly *how* you messed up—maybe you weren't affectionate enough, or didn't express gratitude, or simply said the wrong thing. What matters most is that you're changing your ways—and reassuring your partner that they're valued.

"Always on My Mind" first sprang from the mind of Wayne Carson Thompson (who also goes by Wayne Carson), a songwriter known for penning the Box Tops' hit "The Letter." He happened to be away from home in Memphis, on an extended trip that had run 10 days over, and his wife wasn't thrilled. "She was pretty damned irate about it," Carson told the *Los Angeles Times* in 1988. "So I tried to calm her down. I said, 'Well, I know I've been gone a lot, but I've been thinking about you all the time.'" At this, a lightbulb went off, and he added: "I told her real fast I had to hang up because I had to put that into a song."

However, Carson couldn't figure out how to finish the tune, even after he enlisted songwriting help from a past collaborator, Johnny Christopher. Their savior came in the form of Mark James, who wrote the Elvis Presley–popularized "Suspicious Minds." James overheard the duo working on the song—and realized he knew exactly how to help. According to the *Los Angeles Times*, the trio finally finished it in just four takes.

In 1972 alone, Gwen McCrae, Brenda Lee, and Presley cut "Always on My Mind." But one of the most definitive versions came a decade later, courtesy of country icon Willie Nelson. "'Always on My Mind' bowled me over the moment I first heard it, which is one way I pick songs to record," Nelson shared in his 1988 book, *Willie: An Autobiography.*

In 1982, Nelson and another country legend, Merle Haggard, were recording what would become their collaborative album, *Pancho & Lefty.* During the sessions, producer Chips Moman enlisted none other than Johnny Christopher to play guitar on the record. While in the studio, Christopher sang "Always on My Mind" to Nelson. He was immediately intrigued enough to ponder cutting a duet version with Haggard.

It wasn't meant to be. "Merle didn't particularly like the song," Nelson wrote in *Willie.* "He didn't hear it well enough, I think. As soon as Merle and I finished our album—*Pancho & Lefty*—I stayed in the studio with my band to do a few more tunes. I wanted to see how 'Always on My Mind' would sound with just me singing it." The results were stunning: a gentle ballad brimming with emotion, regret, and humility. Accompanied by wistful piano, understated guitar, and somber backing vocalists, Nelson sounds remorseful but ready to make amends for his own behavior.

This version of "Always on My Mind" was a resounding success. It became Nelson's biggest mainstream pop hit to date, reaching No. 5 on the *Billboard* Hot 100, and topped the Hot Country Singles chart. "Always on My Mind" also won three Grammy Awards, two for the songwriters (Song of the Year and Best Country Song) and one for Nelson (Best Male Country Vocal Performance). For good measure, Nelson's tune also won Song of the Year two years in a row at the Country Music Association Awards.

"Always on My Mind" has remained in Nelson's setlists for decades, although others have also kept the song relevant. Several years after the tune's country success, Pet Shop Boys also had a major hit with a rousing synth-pop cover of the song. It was quite different—although the sentiments still rang true. "Everybody had told me, 'You're not going to like it. They changed some of the melody, they changed a couple of words and they added all these synthesizers and things,'" Carson told the *Los Angeles Times*. "But I just kept an open mind and when I finally heard it, I thought, 'Hell, that's a great record.' I don't think you can hurt a good song, and this is living proof."

TIME AFTER TIME

1983 · CYNDI LAUPER

Songwriters: Rob Hyman and Cyndi Lauper

IN THE EARLY 1980s, Cyndi Lauper hit pop culture like a rainbow-colored hurricane, thanks to her brilliant outfits and upbeat musical confections like "Girls Just Wanna Have Fun." But even then, she had a serious and introspective side—as evidenced by the ballad "Time After Time." Named after a 1979 science fiction movie called *Time After Time* that Lauper saw referenced in *TV Guide*, the song conveys a comforting romantic thought: I'll be there for you through thick and thin, whenever you need me, even if you stumble or we're having relationship troubles.

"Time After Time" was the final tune cut for Lauper's 1983 debut album, *She's So Unusual*, and it represented a collaboration between her and Rob Hyman, the cofounder of Philadelphia rock band the Hooters. Lauper was thrilled to be flexing her songwriting chops, and she and Hyman met in a studio with a Steinway concert grand piano.

According to the *Wall Street Journal*, Hyman started working up a part with a "bouncy, upbeat reggae vibe" based around four chords. "While Rob played, I stood next to the piano and danced, kind of free form," Lauper said. "Moving around like that to the music helped me figure out how the song should feel." To her surprise, she started singing lyrics drawn on images from her personal life: previous romantic relationships, for example, or a loud clock from her then manager/boyfriend Dave Wolff.

Particularly evocative is a verse built around a moment when Lauper sings of walking ahead of her partner; she can't hear him because she's too far away. But when he tells her to slow down, she finally falls back into step, a gesture compared to a watch going haywire. Brilliantly, the song's drums (courtesy of session drummer Anton Fig) sound like a ticking clock at this point in the song—and periodically slip into this rhythm again during other moments that reference the concept of time.

Separately, a transformative musical shift added further depth. "When we slowed it down, the song became heartbreaking," Hyman said. "There was suddenly so much emotion in the song. I was going through some relationship issues and Cyndi had similar experiences, so we both felt it." That translated to heartbeat-like rhythms, pensive keyboards that surged like an ocean wave, and atmospheric guitar from Hyman's bandmate Eric Bazilian. Lauper also tracked one of the most moving vocal performances of her career, one that's deeply felt and rueful.

"Time After Time" reached No. 1 on the *Billboard* Hot 100 and also topped the charts in Canada. Over the years, the song has grown into something of a standard: Miles Davis added it to his live repertoire after recording an instrumental version for 1985's *You're Under Arrest*, while the R&B artist INOJ released a 1998 cover of the song that reached No. 6 on the Hot 100. In 2021, a cover of the song was even used in a McDonald's commercial in the UK.

ISLANDS IN THE STREAM

1983 · DOLLY PARTON AND KENNY ROGERS

Songwriters: Barry Gibb, Maurice Gibb, Robin Gibb

KENNY ROGERS WAS king of the duet in the late 1970s and into the 1980s. Not only did he release two collaborative albums with country icon Dottie West, but he also had hits teaming up with Sheena Easton, Kim Carnes, and Ronnie Milsap. Rogers's biggest duet was with his old pal Dolly Parton: In 1983, the pair joined forces for the indomitable "Islands in the Stream."

A jaunty number about two people realizing they can't—and, more important, *don't want to*—live without each other, "Islands in the Stream" praises the power of a rock-solid love. *Nothing* can come between them—not other people, not suspicion of their relationship, not life's vicissitudes. Instead, the pair share mutual respect (and attraction) and are happy enjoying their time together.

Although the song was written by the Bee Gees—brothers Barry Gibb, Robin Gibb, and Maurice Gibb—the trio hadn't planned on recording it themselves. Instead, "Islands in the Stream" was envisioned as a solo song for Diana Ross or Marvin Gaye. In a 2021 *Billboard* interview, Barry revealed that the tune evolved into its final form when he agreed to produce Rogers's 1983 LP *Eyes That See in the Dark*. Rogers wanted to record a duet with Parton, he noted. "And so we suggested that one—we knew it was good, we knew it was potentially very strong, but we didn't know it was a duet. So we just went to work on that, and the R&B song became a country song."

That it did—and then some. The song exemplified the genre cross-pollination common in the early '80s: Rogers and Parton belted out their earnest parts above soft-glow keyboards, a galloping tempo, and rollicking twang flourishes.

As a result, "Islands in the Stream" became a massive crossover hit that topped the *Billboard* Hot 100, Hot Country Singles, and Adult Contemporary charts *at the same time* for *two straight weeks* in fall 1983.

In later years, "Islands in the Stream" popped up here and there, most notably as a basis for the 1998 Pras, Wyclef Jean, Ol' Dirty Bastard, and Mya collaboration "Ghetto Supastar (That Is What You Are)." The Bee Gees also later covered the tune themselves—and in 2009, Robin Gibb appeared alongside Tom Jones on "(Barry) Islands in the Stream," a UK No. 1 charity benefit single by BBC stars Vanessa Jenkins and Bryn West.

I WANT TO KNOW WHAT LOVE IS

1984 · FOREIGNER

Songwriter: Mick Jones

WHEN BANDS RELEASE an album, they typically release an upbeat tune as the lead single and then save ballads for the second single. Foreigner, however, flouted this trend as they prepared to issue their 1984 LP, *Agent Provocateur*. The album's first single, "I Want to Know What Love Is," was a majestic power ballad distinguished by vocalist Lou Gramm's sensitive, soulful delivery and lyrics laying bare the agony of searching for a lasting love.

Foreigner recorded the song at Right Track Studio in New York City. The band's leader and songwriter, Mick Jones, co-produced the song alongside Alex Sadkin, who had recently experienced success with Duran Duran and Thompson Twins. Fittingly, the latter band's vocalist, Tom Bailey, appeared on "I Want to Know What Love Is," contributing a memorable keyboard part on a Jupiter-8 synthesizer. He wasn't the only big name moonlighting on the tune: Broadway powerhouse Jennifer Holliday also contributed vocals.

But Jones recalled to *Classic Rock* magazine (as quoted via Ultimate Classic Rock) that the gospel-influenced harmonies from the New Jersey Mass Choir elevated the song even more. "We did a few takes, and it was good, but it was still a bit tentative. So then they all got round in a circle, held hands and said 'The Lord's Prayer.' And it seemed to inspire them, because after that they did it in one take. I was in tears, because my mum and dad were in the studio too, and it was so emotional."

As Jones recalled in 2014, writing "I Want to Know What Love Is" was also an emotional experience; in fact, the song poured out of him. "I was almost possessed with trying to dig deep inside me to bring up experiences, ideas, memories—anything that sounded convincing in a song," he said, noting he wrote the song around 2 a.m. "The night the song came about, I was thinking about the basic human emotions we all feel. Once I started to open up to what was moving me, it all happened very quickly."

Incredibly, Jones initially seemed reluctant to share his song with other people. In 1985, former Foreigner vocalist Lou Gramm recalled that his bandmate even "tried to fast-forward" past the song while they were going over cassette demos. "I said, 'Hey, what's that?' and he said, 'Nah, let's move on to something else.'" Gramm understood Jones's hesitation when he finally heard the song. "Lyrically, it was pretty emotional for him. The song represented things in his own life that he hadn't been able to resolve, and he wasn't too sure he wanted to have millions of people hear about it."

Indeed, Jones once told Songfacts that the song did start out from his personal experience. "I'd been through a lot of relationships that eventually failed, and still searching for something that could really endure." He wanted to make the song relatable to everyone. And so in its final form, "I Want to Know What Love Is" is a deeply vulnerable song about realizing you're in love with someone—and being brave enough to reveal your feelings to them. The catch is, there's no guarantee the other person will reciprocate this love; however, the narrator has mulled things over carefully, weighed the pros and cons, and decided taking the risk was worth it.

As it turns out, being vulnerable paid off for Jones and Foreigner: The song topped the pop charts in multiple countries, including Australia, Canada, the US, the UK, and Ireland. It's also been covered by a who's who of vocalists, including Mariah Carey, Tina Arena, and Wynonna Judd.

THE POWER OF LOVE

1985 · HUEY LEWIS AND THE NEWS

Songwriters: Johnny Colla, Chris Hayes, Huey Lewis

MUSIC IS AN integral part of the iconic '80s movie *Back to the Future*. Not only does a pivotal scene with a school dance feature both the Penguins' twinkling hit "Earth Angel (Will You Be Mine)" and Chuck Berry's scorching "Johnny B. Goode," but the film starts with a high-energy opening montage of Marty McFly (Michael J. Fox) heading to school via skateboard. As he hangs on to various moving vehicles to expedite the trip, Huey Lewis and the News' "The Power of Love" blares in the background.

As the title implies, the song is about why love is awesome—when it's good, that is. In some cases, love can be a downer; in other situations, it can make you angry. Love can even be mean or appear unexpectedly. But "The Power of Love" reassures that when you open your heart to love, it can also be transformative. In other words, make sure you use love's power wisely.

Now, Marty McFly's favorite band just happened to be Huey Lewis and the News; in fact, *Back to the Future*'s filmmakers were using the group's 1984 hit "I Want a New Drug" as placeholder music in the movie. Naturally, Huey & Co. were asked to contribute new and original music for the film. There was only one problem, Lewis confessed to The A.V. Club in 2012: "I said, 'Sounds great, but I don't know how to write for film. We write these songs together. We just kind of write them.'" But he did have a tune called "In the Nick of Time" he thought could work.

Unfortunately, that song ended up being used in the film *Brewster's Millions*—Patti LaBelle sang it—and so Huey Lewis and the News went back to work on tunes for *Back to the Future*, coming up with a song called "Back in Time" in addition to "The Power of Love." The latter's title came from a song penned by Alex Call, a former bandmate of Lewis (and the co-writer of Tommy Tutone's "867-5309"); in his memoir, Call notes he was paid for the title but doesn't have a songwriting credit.

Instead, Lewis and guitarist Chris Hayes worked up the tune, and guitarist/saxophonist/co-writer Johnny Colla polished it off with the gigantic, stair-step synth hook. "And what do you know? It became the intro, the chorus, and the outro," Colla told Grantland in 2013. "Chris had written it as lots of moving notes, and I thought, it's gotta be a bit more pop. Something's gotta make it snap. That was my contribution." Buoyed by that riff—and a dynamite combination of smoky Lewis vocals, bar-band horns,

hot-rodding grooves, and a bluesy guitar solo on the bridge—"The Power of Love" sounded unstoppable.

Speaking in *The Billboard Book of Number One Hits*, *Back to the Future* music supervisor Bones Howe notes that "The Power of Love" came in at the very last minute: "We went right up to a couple days before the final mix of the movie before we had the finished version of [the song]." Incredibly enough, Howe added that the tune wasn't universally beloved. "There were a lot of people who were saying, 'It's a terrible record. "Back in Time" is the hit record,'" he recalls. "I said it's a smash, it's a wonderful record."

Howe was proven right: "The Power of Love" spent two weeks at No. 1 on the *Billboard* Hot 100 and heralded great things for *Back to the Future*, which grossed $210 million in the US. Given the enduring affection for both Huey Lewis and the News and the movie—the latter is even now a Broadway musical—the power of love remains very transformative indeed.

CRAZY FOR YOU

1985 • MADONNA

Songwriters: John Bettis and Jon Lind

AFTER BECOMING A massive music star, Madonna didn't take long to branch out into movies. In 1985, she appeared as a nightclub singer in the romantic melodrama *Vision Quest* and portrayed an unconventional bohemian in *Desperately Seeking Susan*. Although the latter film became a hit, the former didn't exactly set the box office ablaze. *Vision Quest* ended up becoming notable for another reason: Madonna's second *Billboard* Hot 100 No. 1 hit, "Crazy for You."

Cut from the same soulful cloth as her previous hit "Borderline," the song is a keening ballad that captures the experience of hitting it off with a stranger in a club. Lyrically, it describes the entire exchange—spotting someone cute across the room, locking eyes with them, initiating a slow dance, and finally consummating the attraction with a kiss. The tension is palpable in the words, particularly in the chorus, which describes the electric feeling of touching someone to whom you're wildly attracted. And, vocally, Madonna nails the passion and longing inherent in such a spicy encounter.

"Crazy for You" was co-written by two songwriters with impressive pedigrees. Jon Lind co-wrote Earth, Wind & Fire's 1979 disco smash "Boogie Wonderland" and later worked with Cher and Vanessa Williams, while John Bettis was a lyricist known for Carpenters hits such as "Top of the World" and "Goodbye to Love" and the Pointer Sisters' "Slow Hand." Despite the fact Madonna was in *Vision Quest*, the duo was actually surprised that she was enlisted to sing the song.

The skepticism is even more curious because the song ended up matching a scene in the film, Bettis was quoted as saying in *The Billboard Book of Number 1 Hits.* "In reading the script, the place I wanted to write a song for was the first time that the two main characters, a young boy and a girl who's a boarder at the house, dance together at a club. We were noodling around and ('Crazy for You') was something that Jon was singing over that section of the song."

Unfortunately, the first pass at cutting "Crazy for You" with producer Phil Ramone wasn't a success. Luckily, however, the single's next producer was noted New York City club DJ John "Jellybean" Benitez, a frequent Madonna collaborator (and paramour) at the time. Jellybean tapped Rob Mounsey to work some magic on the arrangement—which Mounsey told the podcast *80sography* he did by "sort of writing an orchestral arrangement" and then "playing all the parts individually on some keyboards," particularly a Jupiter-8 and Yamaha DX7. For good measure, George Marge contributed soaring oboe, which added just the right melodramatic tone. (The oboe was all Madonna's idea, Mounsey added.)

"Crazy for You" became the first in a long line of Madonna hits tied to movie appearances. And commercially, it endured well beyond *Vision Quest*: After reaching No. 2 in the UK upon its initial release in 1985, the song reached the same peak in 1991 after a slightly remixed version from Madonna's greatest hits album *The Immaculate Collection* became a single.

DON'T YOU (FORGET ABOUT ME)

1985 • SIMPLE MINDS

Songwriters: Keith Forsey and Steve Schiff

LIKE MANY UK bands that started off in the late-'70s punk or post-punk scenes, Simple Minds found success in America during the 1980s by embracing a more mainstream, synth-heavy sound. That was evident on their US breakthrough hit "Don't You (Forget About Me)," which appeared in the iconic teen movie *The Breakfast Club* and brimmed with booming drums, shimmering keyboards, and polished production.

The song's co-writers also toed the line between punk and new wave. Steve Schiff played guitar in the Nina Hagen Band, while Keith Forsey produced Billy Idol's hit *Rebel Yell* LP and won an Oscar for co-writing the 1983 Irene Cara hit "Flashdance . . . What a Feeling." Interestingly enough, "Don't You (Forget About Me)" wasn't meant to be a romantic song about cherished memories—but was instead a song about friendship and fellowship, inspired by Forsey's school days memories and the dynamic between *The Breakfast Club*'s awkward, smart "brain" Anthony Michael Hall and tough-guy "criminal" Judd Nelson.

"When they were away from everybody else, the two of them actually recognised each other," Forsey told *The Guardian*. "That was the reason I came up with 'Don't You (Forget About Me).' It was: Don't forget, when we're back in the classroom, you're not just a bad guy and we've got other things in common."

Finding the right artist to cut this song was a surprisingly difficult task. *The Breakfast Club* co-producer Michelle Manning "literally wandered the streets of London for two-and-a-half, almost three weeks" with music supervisor David Anderle, she told *Spin*. The pair went to "every major English group, with a three-quarter-inch tape of [the movie]" trying to find a suitable band to tackle the song.

Roxy Music front man Bryan Ferry was offered the song but declined due to "bad timing," he told *The Guardian*. "We were finishing off [my solo album] *Boys and Girls*, which was way behind schedule, and we didn't want the distraction." Simple Minds were also courted, but they were reluctant to record other people's songs; even a private showing of the movie reportedly didn't sway them.

Pretenders leader Chrissie Hynde—then married to Simple Minds vocalist Jim Kerr—eventually helped turn the tides. "[She] kept badgering me," Kerr told *The Guardian*. "'I like the song,' she said. 'What's the problem?'" A meeting with Forsey—who had proclaimed his Simple Minds fandom—led to successful studio time, which included Kerr ad-libbing his inimitable "la-la" part at the song's end.

Despite the complicated genesis, this persistence paid off: "Don't You (Forget About Me)" was the perfect song to end *The Breakfast Club* on a triumphant note—and it also ended up becoming Simple Minds' first and only US No. 1 hit. Over the years, it has remained one of the most beloved singles of the 1980s; in 2021, it even returned to the *Billboard* charts after appearing in a Super Bowl ad for the tech company Meta.

TAKE MY BREATH AWAY

1986 · BERLIN

Songwriters: Giorgio Moroder (music); Tom Whitlock (lyrics)

THE 1980S WERE a golden age for movie soundtracks—and movie soundtrack hits. Among the best is Berlin's "Take My Breath Away," which appears in 1986's *Top Gun* as the soundtrack for romantic moments between Tom Cruise (Pete "Maverick" Mitchell) and Kelly McGillis (Charlotte "Charlie" Blackwood). The song captures the delicious anticipation of a sexual dalliance—and the desire that crackles between two people who lust after each other—via airy synths, a seductive bass groove, and steady drums.

Co-writer (and disco maven) Giorgio Moroder was no stranger to movie magic, having co-written and co-produced Blondie's "Call Me" (from *American Gigolo*) and Limahl's worldwide hit "Never Ending Story" (from *The NeverEnding Story*). But he met his "Take My Breath Away" collaborator Tom Whitlock in an unusual way. "My Ferrari was parked behind the studio, with brake trouble," Moroder told *The Guardian*. "One day a guy, Tom Whitlock, came by and said he was a mechanic and could fix it. Later he said: 'Oh and, by the way, I'm also a lyricist. If you ever need some words . . .'" Moroder handed over some demos and Whitlock came back with lyrics for not just "Take My Breath Away" but also another *Top Gun* soundtrack highlight, Kenny Loggins's "Danger Zone."

Finding the right singer took a bit longer. The Motels' Martha Davis demoed the song but ended up not being chosen. (Davis was fine with the decision, writing later in the liner notes of Martha Davis and The Motels' compilation *Anthologyland*: "There's a big part of me that is glad that I didn't do it because I'm a writer and I think I would have been known more for that song than any other.") The synth-driven rock band Berlin was on Moroder's radar because they had been working with him on their song "No More Words," and vocalist Terri Nunn received a nod to try the song.

Fortuitously, Nunn happened to have acting experience—she auditioned to play Princess Leia and turned down the part of Lucy Ewing on *Dallas* to pursue music—which she was able to use while tracking the song. "[Moroder] kept bringing me back to simplify the vocal, saying, 'People need to want to sing along,'" she told *The Guardian*. "In acting, I'd learned a lot about channeling emotion. I was alone. I'd been so busy with the band I'd not had a relationship for four years. So I sang it from a feeling of sadness and longing, and maybe that's what resonated." Indeed, Nunn's performance is glamorous and yearning; she inhabits the song's emotional lyrics perfectly.

"Take My Breath Away" won an Oscar and Golden Globe for Best Original Song and was a top 10 hit around the world, including reaching No. 1 in the US and UK. The single was so popular in the UK that it was reissued twice and reached No. 3 in 1990. Unfortunately, not every member of Berlin has such happy memories about the success of "Take My Breath Away." In a 2022 interview, Berlin founder and guitarist John Crawford noted they didn't even hear the song before it was slotted in for the band's 1986 album, *Count Three & Pray* ("None of us had anything to do with it. I didn't play on it. Nobody played on it.") and acknowledged he "handled [the experience] really, really poorly and immaturely."

For Nunn, however, the song was life-altering—and continues to pay dividends. "Everything changed when that song came out," she told *Spin*. "We got to play in countries that we'd never been to before as a band, that had no interest in Berlin before that. It opened the door to the world for me, and still does, to this day."

IN YOUR EYES

1986 • PETER GABRIEL

Songwriter: Peter Gabriel

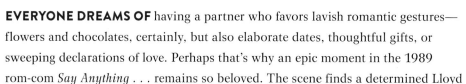

EVERYONE DREAMS OF having a partner who favors lavish romantic gestures—flowers and chocolates, certainly, but also elaborate dates, thoughtful gifts, or sweeping declarations of love. Perhaps that's why an epic moment in the 1989 rom-com *Say Anything . . .* remains so beloved. The scene finds a determined Lloyd Dobler (John Cusack) outside the house of Diane Court (Ione Skye), holding a boombox over his head in an attempt to recapture her heart.

Dobler's overture is doubly iconic because the song blaring out of the radio is Peter Gabriel's "In Your Eyes." On one level, it's a song about a significant other being a North Star, the person you turn to when everything in life seems difficult. All you need to keep going is a deep, soulful look. But on another level, the song explores the gratifying experience of a partner seeing you for who you are. You can let your guard down and be yourself—because through their eyes, you are perfect.

Originally found on his 1986 LP, *So*, the tune "began its life as a love song," Gabriel said in a 2011 video interview. "But I was very interested in this idea that in the West we keep love songs separate from religious songs." This is different from how it was in Africa, he noted, where "sometimes love is something which can be ambiguous. It could be love of a woman, or it could be love of God. So that is what I was trying to explore." Fittingly, with references to churches and light, the lyrics possess a spiritual bent.

Musically, "In Your Eyes" is "built around these African grooves and motifs" Gabriel said in the same video interview. Co-produced by Gabriel along with Bill Laswell and Daniel Lanois, the song combines these elements with plush instrumentation: sensuous synthesizers, evocative piano from session great Richard

Top 10 Heartbreak Songs

1. Adele, "Someone Like You"
2. Little Anthony and the Imperials, "Tears on My Pillow"
3. Boyz II Men, "End of the Road"
4. Toni Braxton, "Un-Break My Heart"
5. The Four Tops, "Baby I Need Your Loving"
6. Natalie Imbruglia, "Torn"
7. Bonnie Raitt, "I Can't Make You Love Me"
8. Roxette, "It Must Have Been Love"
9. Wham!, "Careless Whisper"
10. Hank Williams, "I'm So Lonesome I Could Cry"

Tee, and Tony Levin's liquid bass. Backing vocals come from Simple Minds' Jim Kerr and the Call's Michael Been, while the Senegal-born superstar Youssou N'Dour brings the song home with a touching solo.

Gabriel added that after "In Your Eyes" appeared in *Say Anything* . . . , its meaning became a little less fluid. "A lot of people have ended up getting married to it or having it as a prom song," he said. "It's now become part of people's emotional landscape as well."

"In Your Eyes" wasn't a single in Gabriel's native England but reached No. 26 on the US *Billboard* Hot 100 chart. Thanks to *Say Anything* . . . , it also remains one of the musician's most recognizable songs. "It is one of the modern-day Romeo and Juliet balcony clichés," Gabriel told *Rolling Stone.* "I've talked to John Cusack about that. We're sort of trapped together in a minuscule moment of contemporary culture."

Both men seem at peace with this reputation, however. During a 2012 Gabriel concert at the Hollywood Bowl, Cusack himself even snuck onstage as "In Your Eyes" started and handed over a gigantic boombox—a symbolic gesture that has kept Lloyd Dobler's legacy alive and well.

KISS

1986 · PRINCE AND THE REVOLUTION

Songwriter: Prince

SEDUCTION, THY NAME is Prince. No artist has written more tunes espousing the pleasure of, well, *pleasure*. Sure, that certainly includes sex—but the Purple One also considers foreplay, hedonism, and debauchery to fall under this category.

"Kiss" especially celebrates the fun of getting busy. Prince reassures his lady she doesn't need to have money, boast previous sexual experience, or even be a specific zodiac sign—he just wants to smooch. Mind you, he is *somewhat* picky: Dirty talk and too much flirtation are no-gos, but he wants to be with someone mature who is comfortable in her own skin *and* has an attitude. The overarching message is that everyone is entitled to feel beautiful—and a chance to get freaky in the bedroom.

Although "Kiss" became one of Prince's signature songs, he wasn't originally going to record it, earmarking it instead for a Minneapolis R&B group named Mazarati signed to his label, Paisley Park Records. "Kiss" also didn't *sound* funky at first. Prince's demo was stripped-down, dominated by acoustic guitar and a solemn vibe tinted by the blues. "The song sounded like a folk song that Stephen Stills might have done," producer David Z told *Mix*. "I didn't quite know what to do with it and neither did the group."

In April 1985, David Z and Mazarati took a stab at recording a version—cobbling together a drum machine beat, a piano part nicked from Bo Diddley's "Say Man," a deep lead vocal track, and background vocals developed out of Brenda Lee's "Sweet Nothings." To David Z, the song "was just a collection of ideas built around the idea of a song that wasn't finished yet," he told *Mix*. "We didn't know where it was going."

Enter Prince, who *very clearly* saw the song's potential. Bright and early the next day, he headed to the studio, added guitar and vocals to the song, and made it his own. "I asked him what was going on," David Z said. "He said to me, 'This is too good for you guys. I'm taking it back.'"

Their work wasn't totally for naught: Mazarati's backing vocals ended up making it into the final version of the song that appeared on Prince & the Revolution's 1986 LP, *Parade,* as well as in the movie *Under the Cherry Moon.* But "Kiss" was yet another huge hit for Prince, reaching No. 1 on the *Billboard* Hot 100 and landing in the top 10 in multiple other countries.

EVERYWHERE

1987 · FLEETWOOD MAC

Songwriter: Christine McVie

FLEETWOOD MAC IS often considered to be synonymous with romantic strife. That's mainly due to the band's 1977 LP, *Rumours,* which emerged out of intra-band relationship turmoil. Bassist John McVie and keyboardist/vocalist Christine McVie had divorced, while longtime collaborators/romantic partners Stevie Nicks and Lindsey Buckingham were also breaking up.

But it isn't *entirely* fair to pigeonhole Fleetwood Mac as the patron saints of relationship drama. The songs Christine McVie contributed to the band especially had a more hopeful and loving tone. Take the frothy "Everywhere" from 1987's *Tango in the Night*, which features someone on the precipice of falling in love. In fact, they're so thrilled to have these feelings—and proud to be with their partner— they can't wait to spend every waking moment with them. It's an ideal romantic situation; in other words, being with someone who can't wait to tell everybody their partner is the greatest.

Led by McVie's regal lead vocals, "Everywhere" envelops listeners like a shroud of mist, courtesy of fizzy synthesizers, galloping rhythms, and gauzy backing vocals. "I'm very good at coming up with lyrics, songs and hooks, and Lindsey is very good at making it 3D," McVie once told *Mojo*. That was especially true on "Everywhere," which embodied the contemporary pop-rock direction of *Tango in the Night* and reflected Buckingham's exploration of modern technology (like the Fairlight CMI synth) and penchant for studio perfection. "I loved working with him, because he just brought phenomenal production ideas to my songs and improved them," McVie was quoted as saying in the 2019 documentary *Fleetwood Mac's Songbird: Christine McVie*.

For example, the glittering intro features both acoustic and electric guitars played at a slow speed and then manipulated to sound even more beautiful. "[Lindsey] slowed the tape down, really slowly, and played the parts slowly," McVie explained. "And then when it came to the right speed, it sounded bloody amazing."

The song topped *Billboard*'s Adult Contemporary chart and reached No. 14 on the Hot 100 but was a massive hit in McVie's native England, reaching No. 4 on the charts. Over the years, pop stars Niall Horan and Anne-Marie and the rock band Paramore have covered "Everywhere," while the song has also been used in a popular UK ad. On Fleetwood Mac's final tour, the tune was an upbeat highlight that felt like a ray of warm sunshine.

SWEET CHILD O' MINE

1987 · GUNS N' ROSES

Songwriter: Guns N' Roses

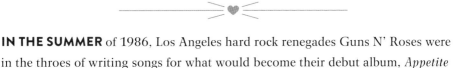

IN THE SUMMER of 1986, Los Angeles hard rock renegades Guns N' Roses were in the throes of writing songs for what would become their debut album, *Appetite for Destruction*. Having traded a beyond-squalid living space dubbed the Hell House for a place on the former estate of filmmaker Cecil B. DeMille, the band was focused on songwriting.

From this environment sprang a very unlikely tune: the tender love song "Sweet Child O' Mine." The narrator is infatuated with a crush, comparing the feeling of being with her to the happy innocence of childhood, as she provides solace and safety. Notably, she also has brilliant blue eyes that compare favorably to a sky, giving the hopeless-romantic narrator a chance to hope that they're never clouded with rain. By the end of the song, the big question is where this couple goes next now that their true feelings are out in the open—although all signs point to a happy ending.

"Sweet Child O' Mine" started off as a *very* loose idea. "I was fucking around with this stupid little riff," guitarist Slash told *Q* magazine in 2005. Guitarist Izzy Stradlin was also there, contributing his own ideas. The resulting music incorporated Slash's guitar riff—a bright, booming electric part that cascaded up and down like a carousel horse—and melodic, bluesy hard rock flourishes that were both yearning and tenacious. Slash also ushers the song out with extended guitar solos that, when paired with vocalist Axl Rose's anguished cries, capture the song's unguarded heart.

At first, the band didn't see the song's brilliance. Slash called it "a very sappy ballad" and shared that fleshing out the tune "was like pulling teeth." Bassist Duff McKagan, meanwhile, added, "It was like a joke. We thought, 'What is this song? It's gonna be nothing.'"

But Rose had overheard the initial guitar jam and was blown away by what he heard. In fact, he was so inspired that he wrote a sweet poem for his then girlfriend, Erin Everly, that explains the heartfelt lyrics. "If Axl hadn't been there writing those lyrics," Slash later told *Rolling Stone*, "chances are that song would have never existed."

Rose was committed to ensuring that "Sweet Child O' Mine" became something special. He even referred to the music of a rather unexpected classic rock band to make sure he nailed the song's sentiment.

"I'm from Indiana, where Lynyrd Skynyrd are considered God to the point that you ended up saying, 'I hate this fucking band!'" Rose told *Sounds* in 1987. "And yet for 'Sweet Child' . . . I went out and got some old Skynyrd tapes to make sure that we'd got that heartfelt feeling."

Mission accomplished. "Sweet Child O' Mine" ended up becoming a huge hit, spending two weeks at No. 1 on the *Billboard* Hot 100—the first and only Guns N' Roses song to reach this peak—and won an American Music Award for Favorite Pop/Rock Song.

WITH OR WITHOUT YOU

1987 · U2

Songwriters: U2

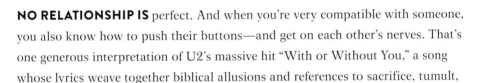

NO RELATIONSHIP IS perfect. And when you're very compatible with someone, you also know how to push their buttons—and get on each other's nerves. That's one generous interpretation of U2's massive hit "With or Without You," a song whose lyrics weave together biblical allusions and references to sacrifice, tumult, and miscommunication.

Perhaps unsurprisingly, Bono called "With or Without You" a "really twisted love song" in a 1987 *Rolling Stone* interview and described the lyrics as "pure torment" in the book *U2 by U2*. The reason for these harsh descriptions might surprise you, however: As it turns out, "With or Without You" might have more to do with internal conflict. "One of the things that was happening at that time was the collision in my own mind between being faithful to your art or being faithful to your lover," Bono explained. "What if the two are at odds? Your gift versus domestic responsibility?"

He clarified that he wasn't necessarily talking about cheating or betrayal—but instead grappling with the freedom to be curious and adventurous. "If I meet somebody and I want to go off with them, to find out what their world is like, I can't because I'm a married man," Bono continued. "It's not even about sexual infidelity, I just remember thinking. 'Is this the life of an artist? Am I going to have kids and settle down and betray my gift or am I going to betray my marriage?'"

U2 had just as much trouble figuring out the song's music, bassist Adam Clayton said in *U2 by U2*. "The chord sequence came from Bono but, in early versions, it sounded very traditional because the chords just went round and round and round. It was hard to find a different take on it or a new way into it, it was just a promise of a song."

In the end, "With or Without You" finally took shape with help from longtime band associate Gavin Friday—who "pulled [the song] out of the wastepaper bin, organized it, structured it and was the one who believed it could be a big hit," Bono said in *U2 by U2*—and a new instrument called the Infinite Guitar. The guitar, which Bono said "makes a beautiful haunting ghost of a guitar sound," meshed perfectly with an existing bass part—and helped the band find a way forward.

With production from Daniel Lanois and Brian Eno and a mix from Steve Lillywhite, "With or Without You" opts to cloak its anguish in gauzy tones—not just the ghostly guitar sounds but rocking-baby rhythms, spacious keyboards, and a thrumming bass. The end result is a song that sounds lonely and longing—capturing the lyrical ache with a gentle touch.

"With or Without You" spent three weeks at No. 1 on the *Billboard* Hot 100 in 1987 and reached the top of the charts in Ireland and Canada. The song's success also contributed to *The Joshua Tree* winning two Grammy Awards, including the prestigious Album of the Year. Over time, "With or Without You" has become one of U2's most enduring and lauded songs. In pop culture, the song ended up playing a pivotal role in a romance on the beloved '90s sitcom *Friends*, as it soundtracked various moments of the relationship between principal characters Ross (David Schwimmer) and Rachel (Jennifer Aniston).

NEVER TEAR US APART

1988 • INXS

Songwriters: Andrew Farriss (music); Michael Hutchence (lyrics)

THROUGHOUT THE 1980S, the Australian sextet INXS became one of the most popular rock bands in the world, thanks to surging anthems such as "Don't Change" and "What You Need." In 1987, however, the group leveled up considerably in global popularity with the multiplatinum smash album *Kick*. Not only did the LP solidify the band's charismatic brew of blues, rock, funk, and new wave, but it also contained the gorgeous, waltzing "Never Tear Us Apart." Driven by arpeggiated strings and a sudsy saxophone solo by Kirk Pengilly, the tune is a testament to the intimacy of a couple that's deeply in love.

Tragically, "Never Tear Us Apart" took on a much sadder meaning after Michael Hutchence's 1997 death; in fact, the tune was played at his funeral. But multi-instrumentalist Andrew Farriss came up with the music during better times, a 1986 INXS world tour. "I sat down on an upright piano and started working on the chords that would eventually become 'Never Tear Us Apart,'" he shared on the occasion of what would have been Hutchence's 60th birthday. "I thought it had potential and asked Michael what he thought of it. He told me he really liked it, so I recorded a blues-style demo for him."

Originally, the song was more up-tempo and sounded like rockabilly icon Gene Vincent—an influence certainly obvious in the twangy guitar riffage that occasionally pops up. But Hutchence had other ideas for the overall shape of the song, he said in the BBC book series *Classic Albums*. "It sounded better and better, slower and slower to me, because it was kind of poignant—stretched."

Accordingly, producer Chris Thomas swapped in majestic strings for piano. And Hutchence was indeed inspired by the music, writing a poetic tune espousing the idea of explosive love at first sight—the kind of eternal bond that develops in an instant and endures over time. The couple are so close that they don't even need to verbalize their feelings; they share this affection almost telepathically.

Farriss called the lyrics "truly inspired. Straight from the heart. I know how much that lyric meant to him. It was a personal love lyric very much in the moment for him." Hutchence concurred, noting in the BBC book series, "We're really proud of this one, because it's hard to write ballads dealing with love and keep them tough, and stop people from waving their hands in the air all the time and lighting their Bics up."

"Never Tear Us Apart" reached No. 7 on the *Billboard* Hot 100 and came in at No. 282 on *Rolling Stone*'s 2021 list of the 500 Greatest Songs of All Time. Multiple artists have also put their own spin on the song. Soul legend Tom Jones teamed up with the pop star Natalie Imbruglia for a dramatic, string-swept version, moody rock band the National tapped into the song's romantic side, and British soul singer Paloma Faith emphasized torchy rock guitars and cabaret piano. Tall Paul reimagined "Never Tear Us Apart" as a high-energy dance tune called "Precious Heart," while INXS themselves rerecorded "Never Tear Us Apart" with guitarist Ben Harper and French vocalist Mylène Farmer.

IT HAD TO BE YOU

1989 · HARRY CONNICK JR.

Songwriters: Isham Jones (music); Gus Kahn (lyrics)

ALL ROM-COMS ARE measured against the 1989 movie *When Harry Met Sally. . . .* Directed by Rob Reiner and written by Nora Ephron, the film explores the friendship-turned-relationship of Sally Albright (Meg Ryan), a lovingly neurotic journalist with a heart of gold, and sarcastic political analyst Harry Burns (Billy Crystal). *When Harry Met Sally . . .* explores dating and friendship with remarkable frankness and examines the many ways couples finally find love.

One of the most iconic rom-coms of all time deserves an equally iconic soundtrack. Enter pianist Harry Connick Jr., who at that point was an up-and-coming artist who had released two well-received albums. Thanks to the recommendation of Blood, Sweat & Tears drummer Bobby Colomby, Reiner tapped Connick Jr. to cut sophisticated jazz standards for the film's soundtrack.

Among these was "It Had to Be You," which dated from the 1920s and was originally written by a pair of frequent collaborators, the composer-lyricist team of Isham Jones and Gus Kahn. Separately, the men were also quite successful. Saxophonist Jones was a lauded band leader who wrote music for the wartime-popularized "We're in the Army Now" and had a hit in 1921 with a recording of the song "Wabash Blues." Kahn, meanwhile, was an equally decorated lyricist who penned the words to notable songs such as "Makin' Whoopee," "Yes Sir, That's My Baby" and "Dream a Little Dream of Me."

Together, Kahn and Jones co-wrote one of the most realistic love songs of all time. The narrator of "It Had to Be You" isn't looking for a model partner. In fact, they explicitly say they *don't* want someone perfect and even *prefer* it if someone is (occasionally) mean, irritable, or overbearing. They're eager to love someone despite these faults; in their eyes, being with someone who provokes strong emotions is far more exciting than being with someone bland.

The Isham Jones Orchestra recording of "It Had to Be You" became a hit in 1924; fittingly, the label of the shellac disc release noted explicitly, in writing, that the tune was "For Dancing." Over the years, the song was subsequently covered dozens of times, notably by Ginger Rogers and Cornel Wilde, Ray Charles, and Diane Keaton.

Connick Jr. cut two different versions of "It Had to Be You"—one with big band orchestration and vocals and one as an instrumental trio—with bassist Benjamin Jonah Wolfe and drummer Jeff "Tain" Watts. With its robust brass, spiraling strings, and twinkling piano, the big band version sounds plucked straight from the days of Old Hollywood. Connick, Jr. is the perfect person to steer this version, as he sounds like a suave player. The perky instrumental version, meanwhile, allowed the musician to show off his jazz bona fides, as it's a snappy take that feels suited to a velvet-draped lounge.

Fittingly, Connick Jr.'s *When Harry Met Sally . . .* soundtrack was a rousing success, reaching No. 1 on *Billboard*'s Top Jazz Albums chart and winning a Grammy for Best Jazz Male Vocal Performance. The release set him on the path to a successful career in music *and* acting—in fact, in the following years, he balanced his touring work with roles in movies and TV shows.

RIGHT HERE WAITING

1989 · RICHARD MARX

Songwriters: Bruce Gaitsch and Richard Marx

IT'S OFTEN SAID that absence makes the heart grow fonder. But the writer of that proverb certainly wasn't considering long-distance relationships. Maintaining one of these romances is emotionally draining because it's agonizing being separated from a loved one.

That dull ache permeates Richard Marx's "Right Here Waiting," a ballad that appears on 1989's *Repeat Offender*. The Chicago native wrote the song for his future wife Cynthia Rhodes, an actress who was in South Africa shooting a film. "We were not married then and I wanted to meet her because I had not seen her for a few months," he told the *Indian Express* in 2010. "But my visa application was rejected and when I came back, I wrote this song which was more of a letter from me to her."

Unsurprisingly, he wrote the emotional song very quickly, in roughly 20 minutes. Lyrically, "Right Here Waiting" paralleled what he was going through being so far apart from Rhodes. The song's protagonist laments being separated from their love by an ocean, and notes how painful it feels only connecting via phone. At another point, they even wonder if the relationship can survive this distance. In the end, all the narrator can offer is

reassurance that they'll be ready and waiting for their love—no matter *where* life takes the couple next.

Marx intended "Right Here Waiting" to be a private thing between him and Rhodes. He did offer Barbra Streisand first dibs on recording the tune, as the legend had actually enlisted Marx to write her a song. "It was such a personal song to me at the time that I had no intention of recording it," Marx told CBS's *The Talk* in 2021. "I was like, 'I'll give Barbra Streisand "Right Here Waiting"; I'm not gonna do anything with it.'"

He sent over the song and heard back from Streisand almost right away that she liked "Right Here Waiting"—but there was a problem. "I still have this voice mail," Marx recalled, "and it says, 'Richard, I heard the song; it's a beautiful song, but I'm gonna need you to rewrite the lyrics because I'm not gonna be right here waiting for anyone.'"

With Streisand out of the picture, Marx recorded his own version. Composer Jeffrey "C.J." Vanston contributed swooning keyboards and arrangements, while the song's co-writer Bruce Gaitsch added an evocative flamenco acoustic guitar solo on the bridge. Marx, meanwhile, poured his heart and soul into the vocals, channeling his own pain into a genuinely moving performance.

"Right Here Waiting" spent three weeks at No. 1 on the *Billboard* Hot 100 in 1989. A decade later, the R&B singer Monica did her own heartfelt take on the tune, breathing new life into the song. No wonder Marx is so grateful Streisand opted to pass on his song. "She actually did me a solid, because had she not rejected it, I probably would never have recorded it," he told *The Talk*. "And every once in a while I put my arm around her and I say, 'Thank you so much for rejecting my song!'"

THE BEST

1989 • TINA TURNER

Songwriters: Mike Chapman and Holly Knight

TINA TURNER CLOSED out her meteoric 1980s comeback with, appropriately enough, a song called "The Best." A towering power ballad with icy keyboards, crunchy electric guitars, and a stirring saxophone solo by Edgar Winter, the single found Turner bearing her soul—and telling someone that they're better than everyone else in her life. She can't pinpoint just one thing that's the best either. *Everything* about them is the best—their heart, their eyes, what they say, being in their arms. The only thing that isn't amazing? Being away from them.

Given Turner's emphatic delivery and urgent tone, it's a safe assumption that "The Best" is about a person. The song's co-writer, Holly Knight, told Songfacts that the tune is more ambiguous than you might think. "It can be so many things, and that's why it has taken on a life of its own. It can be a love song. It can be love for anything, as Tina [has] said . . . When you've finally found something that's the masterpiece of whatever it is, 'The Best' really describes that."

Knight, who also had a hand in writing Pat Benatar's "Invincible" and songs for Heart, penned "The Best" with Mike Chapman. Separately, the latter had produced hit LPs for Blondie and the Knack. Together, however, Chapman and Knight specialized in co-writing empowering songs—for example, another Turner hit, 1984's "Better Be Good to Me" (with Nicky Chinn) and Pat Benatar's "Love Is a Battlefield."

Surprisingly, "The Best" wasn't an immediate success. Knight originally wrote the tune for the British blue-eyed soul singer Paul Young, who passed on recording it. The song was then recorded by another soulful singer, Bonnie Tyler. Released in 1988, her take on "The Best" charted for only one week in the UK. "I thought,

'That's it—the song's kinda over,'" Knight told Music Business Worldwide in 2023. "Then someone got the song to Tina. So, 'The Best' was not written for Tina Turner, but it was meant for her."

Indeed, Turner quite literally made the song her own, co-producing it with Dan Hartman (of "I Can Dream About You" fame) and even asking Knight to make an important change: writing a bridge. "[She said] 'It is missing a bridge and I want the key to go up after that, then I'll cut the song,'" Knight told Songfacts. "And she was right; that's when it became a hit."

"The Best" peaked at No. 15 on the *Billboard* Hot 100 but became a much bigger hit around the world, recharting several times over the years. In 1992, Turner recorded a duet version of the song with beloved Australian singer Jimmy Barnes, propelling the song to the top 20 in Australia and New Zealand, while "The Best" also reached No. 1 in Scotland in 2010 after the country's Rangers Football Club won the Scottish Premier League title. "It's crazy how, 35 or 40 years later, it's taken on a life of its own," Knight told Music Business Worldwide. "I have never met anyone in any country that doesn't know that song."

FRIDAY I'M IN LOVE

1992 • THE CURE

Songwriters: Perry Bamonte, Simon Gallup, Robert Smith, Porl Thompson, Boris Williams

IN THE LATE 1980s, the Cure achieved mainstream success in the US with the single "Lovesong," which reached No. 2 on the *Billboard* Hot 100. On paper, the placement was unexpected: The moody UK rockers were massively popular in alternative rock circles but were quite unlikely pop stars. Band figurehead Robert

Smith favored black clothes, smeared lipstick, and bedhead, while sonically, the Cure hewed toward the darker side of life.

Despite its gothic-romantic vibe, "Lovesong" was far from melancholy; instead, it was a quite sincere romantic ballad through and through, written by Smith as a wedding gift for his wife, Mary. In a 2008 interview, Smith acknowledged that having a balance between light and dark was important. "There is a small part of what we do that is quite dark in contemporary music terms," he said. "It is quite desolate, there is no hope and I love that side of what we do, but I also realize that if that's all we did then we'd be fucking awful."

Enter the upbeat "Friday I'm in Love." Dubbed "a very naive, happy type of pop song" by Smith, the tune illustrates the power of positive thinking. You can mope around all week and think that your love life is doomed—but on Friday, hope springs eternal because a new week is dawning and so all things are possible. To emphasize this point, Smith uses playful language—for example, rhyming "black," "heart attack," and "back"—and inserts a bridge that describes all the cute little details that make your significant other adorable.

Musically, it's light by the Cure's standards, courtesy of dizzying guitar chords that whirl around like a merry-go-round and Smith's flirtatious vocals. Incredibly enough, by Smith's assessment, the song "is not a work of genius," he said in 2008. "It was almost a calculated song. It's a really good chord progression, I couldn't believe no one else had used it." In fact, Smith started asking people if they recognized the song because he thought there was no chance it was original: "[I thought,] 'I must have stolen this from somewhere, I can't possibly have come up with this.'"

But "Friday I'm in Love" was absolutely a Smith original—and it continued the Cure's commercial hot streak, reaching No. 18 on the *Billboard* Hot 100 and topping the magazine's Modern Rock Tracks chart, while also peaking in the top 10 in the UK and Canada.

I WILL ALWAYS LOVE YOU

1992 • WHITNEY HOUSTON

Songwriter: Dolly Parton

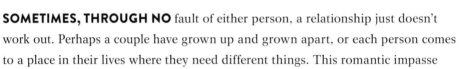

SOMETIMES, THROUGH NO fault of either person, a relationship just doesn't work out. Perhaps a couple have grown up and grown apart, or each person comes to a place in their lives where they need different things. This romantic impasse doesn't necessarily diminish the love between two people or make a breakup any easier. But it still stings.

Dolly Parton wrote "I Will Always Love You" in 1973 on the occasion of a big change: She had decided to leave *The Porter Wagoner Show*, the TV variety show that had launched her career. In a 2015 conversation with the Nashville Songwriters Association International's Bart Herbison, Parton says she recalled asking herself, "How am I gonna make him understand how much I appreciate everything but that I have to go?" She knew the answer, of course: "I went home and I thought, 'Well, what do you do best? You write songs.'"

"I Will Always Love You" arrived quickly, and the very next day, Parton played the song for Wagoner. He started to cry, she recalled. "When I finished, he said, 'Well, hell! If you feel that strong about it, just go on—providing I get to produce that record because that's the best song you ever wrote.'"

That's a pretty big compliment, especially considering Parton's impressive songwriting catalog. But "I Will Always Love You" shines because of its direct, concise lyrics. Parton's narrator is firm but kind as they declare their intention to leave—and leave on good terms. Sure, they acknowledge that the departure is tough, but they also point out the couple is better off apart.

Top 10 Sexy Love Songs

1. 112, "Peaches & Cream"
2. Marvin Gaye, "Let's Get It On"
3. Ginuwine, "Pony"
4. Chris Isaak, "Wicked Game"
5. LL Cool J, "Doin' It"
6. George Michael, "I Want Your Sex"
7. Sade, "The Sweetest Taboo"
8. Bruce Springsteen, "I'm on Fire"
9. Donna Summer, "Love to Love You Baby"
10. Barry White, "Can't Get Enough of Your Love, Babe"

More importantly, they wish their (soon-to-be-former) partner well, both now and in the future, and emphasize that the couple's love is forever. In other words, "I Will Always Love You" initiates an amicable breakup. Accompanied by lullaby-like guitars and twangy pedal steel, Parton sounds nostalgic as she delivers all of this news. A spoken-word bridge where she whispers best wishes is even more wrenching, as she adopts a conspiratorial tone that drips with sadness.

Fittingly, "I Will Always Love You" topped the *Billboard* country charts twice, first in 1974 and then in 1982; the latter, a rerecorded version for the soundtrack to *The Best Little Whorehouse in Texas*, also crossed over to the pop chart, reaching No. 53.

A decade later, "I Will Always Love You" became an even bigger pop hit, spending 14 weeks atop the *Billboard* Hot 100. This version wasn't recorded by Parton but by superstar Whitney Houston for her film debut in *The Bodyguard*. (Interestingly enough, John Doe of the punk band X also recorded a version heard in the movie when Houston and her costar Kevin Costner dance together.) Houston's take also employs sparse instrumentation, in the form of pensive keyboards and a longing-filled saxophone solo. And the vocal powerhouse also gave one of her best performances ever, amplifying the heartache in the song by deliberately teasing out the nuances of individual lyrics.

Of particular note is what happens at the song's denouement: Houston pauses and then goes for a skyscraping high note as she sings the titular phrase, slipping into an anguished howl that eventually dissolves into grief and wistfulness. Given the stunning performance, Houston won the Grammy Award for Record of the Year, and her version of the single eventually became one of the all-time best-selling singles ever released by a woman.

COME UNDONE

1993 • DURAN DURAN

Songwriters: Duran Duran

INDIVIDUALS IN A long-term relationship protect each other from stormy elements, ensuring that these partnerships resemble a tranquil sanctuary. That's the overarching theme threading through Duran Duran's 1993 hit "Come Undone." The song starts with some lovely compliments; among other things, the narrator says their partner is like a dream come to life. Then "Come Undone" moves into even more romantic territory: reassurance that if someone comes undone—in other words, makes themselves vulnerable and falls apart—they'll have a soft landing. Even though the outside world might seem harsh—or the relationship itself might occasionally hit bumpy territory—the narrator will always be there providing solace.

Duran Duran vocalist Simon Le Bon wrote the lyrics of "Come Undone" as a birthday present for his wife, supermodel Yasmin Le Bon (née Parvaneh). The couple met in the mid-1980s after Le Bon saw photos of Yasmin in a photographer's portfolio—and managed to procure the phone number of Yasmin's modeling agency. Via this agency, he asked her to go to the movie premiere for 1984's *Indiana Jones and the Temple of Doom.* "It was a really rock star thing to do," Le Bon later told *People.* Yasmin was initially wary about the invitation but agreed to go after a fellow model, Joanne Russell, vouched for Simon and his character.

A whirlwind romance eventually led to the couple getting married in late 1985. Believe it or not, the ceremony was "quiet," Simon told *Smash Hits.* "Just basically a registry office wedding—very straightforward and discreet—with a few friends and relations." The couple went on to have three children and are still married nearly 40 years later.

"Come Undone" is equally timeless. Nudged forward by an undulating rhythm indebted to trip-hop—including a languid drum loop that's an original creation, not a sample of the Soul Searchers' "Ashley's Roachclip," as has been widely reported—as well as rippling keyboards and guitars, the music feels like a slinky slow dance.

The vocals on "Come Undone" are also passionate—not just Le Bon's soulful, tender croon but also a striking backing part from session vocalist Tessa Niles. "My initial idea for the female vocal was quite soft and breathy and sexy," she told *Rolling Stone* in 2020. "I think at one point, [keyboardist] Nick [Rhodes] said, 'Listen, unleash the diva. Just go for it. Bring her out and let's see what you got.'" Enter a performance that provides a passionate vocal counterpoint to Le Bon's lead.

"Come Undone" was a big hit for Duran Duran, reaching No. 7 on the *Billboard* Hot 100 and No. 13 in the UK. It's remained a staple of the band's live setlists to this day. And, in a nod to the everlasting love behind the song, Le Bon later sang "Come Undone" during an impromptu jam at the summer 2023 wedding of James Taylor, the son of Duran Duran drummer Roger Taylor.

COME TO MY WINDOW

1993 · MELISSA ETHERIDGE

Songwriter: Melissa Etheridge

ONE OF THE oldest romantic tropes is a window visit from a beloved. It's seen in the Brothers Grimm fairy tale about Rapunzel: Imprisoned in a tower by a cruel sorceress, the fair maiden lets down her long blond hair so a prince can visit her by climbing through a window. In movies and TV shows, meanwhile, romantic crushes initiate secret trysts by sneaking into bedrooms via windows.

Given this, it's no wonder Melissa Etheridge's passionate "Come to My Window" struck a chord with so many people. The song starts with someone asking their partner to come over, climb through the window, and wait until they get home, implying that a romantic reunion is imminent. From there, "Come to My Window" describes the anguish of a couple trying to maintain a long-distance relationship. Being apart is simply too painful because the emotional intensity of their love is overwhelming.

Augmented by ace session players—including electric guitarist Waddy Wachtel, bassist Pino Palladino, and onetime Stooges and Tom Petty keyboardist Scott Thurston—Etheridge melded her folksy heartland vibe with forceful rock 'n' roll heft. The result is a strident midtempo song brimming with conviction and urgency.

"Come to My Window" appeared on Etheridge's 1993 multiplatinum album, *Yes I Am*, and reached No. 25 on the *Billboard* Hot 100 and No. 4 on the Adult Contemporary chart. *Yes I Am* arrived at a pivotal time in the rocker's life: Etheridge had come out as a lesbian at the Triangle Ball, a January 1993 gala inaugural ball for President Bill Clinton cohosted by the National Gay and Lesbian Task Force and other LGBTQ organizations.

Unsurprisingly, "Come to My Window" also became a queer anthem. The bridge of the song implies that people disapprove of the relationship at the heart of the song—although the couple in question is undeterred, deeply in love, and determined to stay together. "The gay community lifted me up and supported me," Etheridge has said. "That bridge in the song was taken to an anthem level. It bypassed any meaning I ever put in the song and became part of a mass consciousness. It is still a huge moment when I perform it live."

But in her 2002 memoir, *The Truth Is . . .* , Etheridge wrote that the tune "has always been perceived as a love song, but it is really a song about being frustrated." Later in the book, she gave more details, noting that she and her then girlfriend Julie Cypher had hit a rough patch in their relationship, in the form of constant disagreements and long-distance fights over the phone. "This is a very veiled song. It's all about the troubles I was having at home."

With this context, lyrics that seem loving take on a more subdued meaning. For example, a reference to calling a partner just to hear them breathe—which feels like a romantic move—refers to Etheridge's desperation to have a phone call not end in discord, she wrote. "I would have done anything not to fight, even if it meant listening to her silence." And the window-referencing chorus? Well, Etheridge clarified that it was also not romantic: "I was telling her that we can't meet and talk in an adult fashion. We have to meet on the side and talk."

I'D DO ANYTHING FOR LOVE (BUT I WON'T DO THAT)

1993 • MEAT LOAF

Songwriter: Jim Steinman

THE VAST MAJORITY of love songs are clear-cut for a very good reason. When you're expressing your undying affection to a significant other, you want to be straightforward so your intentions aren't misunderstood. One major exception to this rule? Meat Loaf's mystifying smash "I'd Do Anything for Love (But I Won't Do That)," which appeared on the album *Bat Out of Hell II: Back into Hell*.

Unless you're reading the song lyrics *very* closely, it's not necessarily clear what the parenthetical "won't do that" refers to—or that "I'd Do Anything for Love (But I Won't Do That)" is indeed a love song. Among other things, they'll *never* stop dreaming of their beloved and they *won't* forgive themselves if the couple declines to consummate their relationship. Of course, even if you do a careful analysis, it takes a few close reads to realize what the narrator's talking about. During a long-ago TV performance, Meat Loaf even once drilled down into the song's meaning with a chalkboard and pointer, as if he was a college professor giving a lecture.

This complexity shouldn't be a surprise, as Meat Loaf songs are known for being the Greek epic poems of music. Working closely with the songwriter Jim Steinman, the artist born Marvin Lee Aday created some of the most ambitious rock music ever, starting with 1977's *Bat Out of Hell*—home to the multimovement song "Paradise by the Dashboard Light"—and continuing on *Bat Out of Hell II: Back into Hell*. (For good measure, there's a third album in the trilogy as well, 2006's *Bat Out of Hell III: The Monster Is Loose*.)

Writing on his website, Steinman likened "I'd Do Anything for Love (But I Won't Do That)" to "a 'Beauty and the Beast' kind of story." It's a fair comparison: Confusing sentence construction aside, the tune is a majestic romantic fairy tale in which a woman looking for a better life finds her prince. Meat Loaf trades off vocals with the powerful Lorraine Crosby, bringing the song's dramatic imagery and sentiments to life.

Musically, the song is pure Steinman cinematic bombast—a very good thing, indeed. Pounding piano (courtesy of Roy Bittan, on loan from the E Street Band) and gigantic drums by powerhouse player Kenny Aronoff collide with blazing guitars and synths, as well as backing vocals from Todd Rundgren, Kasim Sulton, and Rory Dodd. (The latter also provides memorable vocals on Bonnie Tyler's take on Steinman's "Total Eclipse of the Heart," a love song for vampires.)

In Steinman's eyes, "I'd Do Anything for Love (But I Won't Do That)" was quite easy to understand. "What he 'won't do' is said about six times in the song very specifically," he wrote on his website—although he did admit the song "is a little puzzle," albeit with earnest intentions. "They're all great things: 'I won't stop doing beautiful things and I won't do bad things,'" he wrote. "I'm very proud of that song because it's very much like out of the world of Excalibur. To me, it's like Sir Lancelot or something—very noble and chivalrous."

Meat Loaf channeled this nobility like a champ, and "I'd Do Anything for Love (But I Won't Do That)" became one of 1993's biggest hits, spending five weeks at No. 1 on the *Billboard* Hot 100 and seven weeks at No. 1 on the UK's Official Singles Chart. Meat Loaf also took home a Grammy Award for Best Rock Vocal Performance, Solo—and the song ended up making the list of *Billboard*'s top 100 songs of the entire 1990s. And today, people are also still debating the meaning of "I'd Do Anything for Love (But I Won't Do That)"—the song's Wikipedia page even has a section header titled "Perceived ambiguity of 'that.'"

I'LL MAKE LOVE TO YOU

1994 • BOYZ II MEN

Songwriter: Babyface

KENNY EDMONDS (aka Babyface) grew up as a hopeless romantic, although he was modest about how this translated to his creative pursuits. "To know me personally, I don't think people would say 'He's so emotional' or 'He's very touching,'" he said in a 1995 interview. "It's not like I sit around like I'm a poet and say beautiful things all the time. But when I sit down to write a song, that's when it comes out."

Babyface wrote and produced "I'll Make Love to You" for Boyz II Men, whom he called a "dream group" because they meshed well with his respectful vibe and nonexplicit approach to romance. "They're one of the few groups who can do a song like 'I'll Make Love to You' and they'll come off sincere," he told the *Ottawa Citizen*, adding, "With Boyz II Men, their image and stuff is such that they can say things more subtly."

Indeed, "I'll Make Love to You" is a slow, sensual seduction that exudes respect for women. The song first sets a romantic mood—blowing out a candle and making a wish, a glass of wine, a roaring fire—and then moves on to its core message: The narrator is there to satisfy the whims and desires of his lady. Whatever she wants, she gets—in the form of tenderness, passion, lovemaking, affection, and much, much more. Her wishes are the only things that matter—and *she's* calling the shots as to how this marathon all-night celebration unfolds.

Babyface was correct that Boyz II Men was the perfect group to record "I'll Make Love to You." The Philly quartet excelled at R&B slow jams—courtesy of their multipart harmonies, emotional vocal solos, and intuitive knack for emphasizing certain lyrics—and had already had a monster hit with 1992's "End of the Road," which spent 13 weeks at No. 1 on the *Billboard* Hot 100. But Boyz II Men also nailed the earnest intent and romantic boldness of "I'll Make Love to You"—and there was nothing cheesy *or* sleazy about the way they sang about making love.

"I'll Make Love to You" was another massive hit that spent a staggering 14 weeks at No. 1 on the *Billboard* Hot 100 and also won a Grammy Award for Best R&B Performance by a Duo or Group with Vocals, and two American Music Awards. It also landed at No. 3 on *Billboard*'s overall list of Hot 100 singles of the 1990s.

CAN YOU FEEL THE LOVE TONIGHT

1994 • ELTON JOHN

Songwriters: Elton John (music); Tim Rice (lyrics)

STARTING IN THE late 1980s, Disney had an amazing run of original animated films—a list that includes *The Little Mermaid, Beauty and the Beast, Aladdin*, and *The Lion King*. The latter movie was a bona fide blockbuster: It has grossed nearly $1 billion since its release.

The Lion King's music is also remarkable, led by "Can You Feel the Love Tonight." Composer Tim Rice's lyrics first and foremost capture the quiet tranquility of the end of the day—the time when it's just two people in love together alone, while the rest of the world falls away. But "Can You Feel the Love Tonight" also stresses that love is an equalizer: It's a uniting and universal experience, able

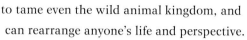

to tame even the wild animal kingdom, and can rearrange anyone's life and perspective. John's music is fittingly lullaby-like, with swooning strings and gentle piano preserving the precious atmosphere described in the song. On the single, backing vocals came from Kiki Dee—famous also for duetting with John on 1976's disco classic "Don't Go Breaking My Heart"—as well as '80s star Rick Astley and Take That's Gary Barlow.

John's take plays over the movie's credits. In the film itself, another version of "Can You Feel the Love Tonight" appears over a scene featuring the lion sweethearts Nala and Simba. Vocally, the majestic felines are represented by (respectively) Sally Dworsky and Joseph Williams—the latter is also the lead singer of Toto—while Kristle Edwards contributes the iconic, soaring solo. Here, "Can You Feel the Love Tonight" has slightly different lyrics that help move the film's storyline along, in addition to extra commentary from the goofball duo of meerkat Timon (Nathan Lane) and warthog Pumbaa (Ernie Sabella). As it turns out, the pair is distressed that they might lose their lion pals to romance.

Incredibly enough, "Can You Feel the Love Tonight" almost appeared in *The Lion King* as a *duet* between Timon and Pumbaa—not as the soundtrack to youthful lion love. In fact, Sabella told CinemaBlend that a full version of the Timon-Pumbaa pairing even exists but was nixed for artistic reasons. "It didn't show up because Elton John said—and it's on film so I can say it—he said, 'I don't want a big, stinky warthog singing my love song!' I love it."

John's insistence that the song stay more serious was a good move. His version reached No. 4 on the *Billboard* Hot 100 and spent eight weeks at No. 1 on the Adult Contemporary chart. His "Can You Feel the Love Tonight" also won an Academy Award for Best Original Song and a Golden Globe Award for Best Original Song; for good measure, John also earned a Grammy Award for Best Male Pop Vocal Performance.

Decades later, the song continues to resonate. For example, Beyoncé covered "Can You Feel the Love Tonight" alongside Donald Glover in the 2019 remake of *The Lion King.* Bey voiced Nala, while Glover portrayed Simba. And a 2020 survey of more than 5,000 people worldwide found that "Can You Feel the Love Tonight" was the best predictor of an enduring partnership: A whopping 77 percent of people who used John's tune as their first dance song stayed married.

BECAUSE YOU LOVED ME

1996 • CELINE DION

Songwriter: Diane Warren

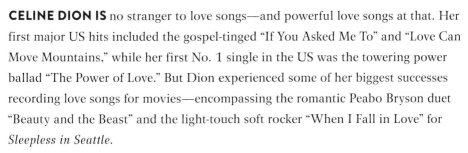

CELINE DION IS no stranger to love songs—and powerful love songs at that. Her first major US hits included the gospel-tinged "If You Asked Me To" and "Love Can Move Mountains," while her first No. 1 single in the US was the towering power ballad "The Power of Love." But Dion experienced some of her biggest successes recording love songs for movies—encompassing the romantic Peabo Bryson duet "Beauty and the Beast" and the light-touch soft rocker "When I Fall in Love" for *Sleepless in Seattle.*

"Because You Loved Me" was the theme song from the 1996 romantic drama *Up Close & Personal*, which costarred Robert Redford and Michelle Pfeiffer. And while the film drew mixed reviews, Dion's tune was a bulletproof highlight. Penned by Diane Warren—who wrote or co-wrote some of the biggest hits of the '80s and '90s, including movie soundtrack highlights such as Starship's "Nothing's Gonna

Stop Us Now"—"Because You Loved Me" praises a balanced relationship that's all possible because of love.

The song's lyrics describe someone gushing over a partner who's empowering and supportive—the kind of person who provides guidance, help, and optimism before even being asked. Need someone to speak up on your behalf or be strong for you? This partner's always game—in fact, it's how they express love. Best of all, the narrator has deep gratitude for this no-questions-asked support; they don't take their partner or their behavior for granted.

In 1997, Warren told *American Songwriter* that although she wrote "Because You Loved Me" specifically for *Up Close & Personal*, she was also inspired by her father, an insurance salesman who had passed away in the late 1980s. "Even though it wasn't written about my dad, emotionally, part of the time in that song, I was there. Part of you can't help but come through in what you are writing."

Dion and Warren had crossed paths before; Warren also wrote "If You Asked Me To." But Dion was an even better fit for "Because You Loved Me." Her vocal performance was nuanced, full of reverence and adoration, which suited the subtle R&B grooves and heartfelt balladry. "I just love writing a great ballad, something so essential that it reaches across genres," Warren told the *Chicago Tribune*. "You could almost say the best songs are genre-transcendent. They translate well into a variety of styles sung by different artists."

Although *Up Close and Personal* didn't end up making the awards show circuits, "Because You Loved Me" was a rousing success. The song was nominated for several Grammys—including big categories like Record of the Year and Song of the Year—and ended up winning Best Song Written for Visual Media. For good measure, Warren was also nominated for an Oscar and Golden Globe in the category of Best Original Song.

ALL MY LIFE

1997 · K-CI & JOJO

Songwriters: Joel "JoJo" Hailey and Rory Bennett

THE 1990S PRODUCED an abundance of classic hip-hop and R&B love songs. Inspired by the massive mainstream success of Babyface and Boyz II Men, artists such as Dru Hill, SWV, P.M. Dawn, and Usher made the charts a more romantic place to be. As the decade progressed, this trend showed no signs of abating. In fact, chances are good that if you went to a prom in the late 1990s, you slow-danced to K-Ci & JoJo's "All My Life." Driven by poignant piano, a languid groove, and the duo's lovely harmonies, it's a quintessential R&B slow jam brimming with romantic sweet nothings.

The duo—brothers Cedric "K-Ci" Hailey and Joel "JoJo" Hailey—were also part of the R&B group Jodeci, which had a string of hits in the early to mid-1990s. But when the pair split off and did their own thing, they decided to go in a slightly different lyrical direction. "We wanted this album to be innocent, to be an album that everyone can listen to and see another side of us," K-Ci told *Billboard* about their debut album, *Love Always.* He later elaborated on what he meant, noting that K-Ci and JoJo's music was definitely more PG-rated.

"With Jodeci, we might sing 'Freek'n You,' and with K-Ci & JoJo, we don't use the word 'sex' one time on the [whole album]," he told *Billboard*. "Jodeci also did love songs like 'Forever My Lady,' 'Love U 4 Life,' and 'Do You Believe in Love.' So we haven't changed, we just calmed it down a little bit."

"All My Life" especially lived up to this family-friendly theme, as JoJo told *Ebony* he originally wrote "All My Life" for his seven-year-old daughter and explained that he wanted the song to have wide appeal. "We want to write songs that women can listen to. You can listen to this in the car, riding with the folks."

It's clear the song evolved beyond that initial inspiration, as the tune's narrator praises a lover for being sweet and precious and says they prayed to find someone so special. The protagonist goes on to swear they'll remain faithful to their partner and expresses deep gratitude for both their beaming smile and unwavering support.

Given the subject matter and unstoppable groove, "All My Life" became hugely popular. The single pulled off the rare feat of hitting No. 1 on both the pop and R&B charts, spending three weeks atop the former and two on the latter, and received Grammy nominations for Best R&B Vocal Performance by a Duo or Group with Vocal and Best R&B Song.

TRULY MADLY DEEPLY

1997 • SAVAGE GARDEN

Songwriters: Darren Hayes and Daniel Jones

WHEN YOU SAY you love someone "truly, madly, deeply," it's a strong statement. The connotation is *urgency*: This isn't some love that you're settling for, but a love that's passionate and enduring. Fittingly, Savage Garden's 1997 ballad "Truly Madly Deeply" describes romantic fireworks. The narrator is smitten with his beloved and promises to fulfill every one of their physical and emotional needs. It doesn't matter where the couple is spending time—for example, standing on a mountain or frolicking in the sea—because life is simply better when they're together.

In its final form, "Truly Madly Deeply" is mellow, with lush keyboards, candle-flicker guitar licks, and glacial production. The song dates to Savage Garden's first demo cassette—albeit in a slightly different form. "The verses were exactly the same, but I'm rather embarrassed to admit the chorus did not exist," Darren Hayes told *Billboard*. "Instead, I'd written a rather awful lyric about magical kisses."

Despite the cringeworthy sentiments, Hayes and Daniel Jones—along with producer Charles Fisher—saw potential in the music. And so, the night before Savage Garden was done recording their 1997 self-titled debut album, Hayes revisited the song. While drinking coffee by himself in a café in Sydney, Australia, he finally landed on the right chorus and finished the tune. Hayes titled the song after the 1990 movie *Truly, Madly, Deeply*, noting in *The Billboard Book of Number One Hits*, "It was a 'wink-wink nudge-nudge' reference to a film I didn't think anyone had seen."

Speaking to *Billboard* in 2011, Hayes shared more about his inspiration. "All I can tell you is that I was in love and missing my love so much it hurt when I wrote the lyrics," he said. "I remember thinking there must have been something in the DNA of the song that anyone in love can relate to. It's simple, incredibly simple melodically. Yet it's kind of timeless."

"Truly Madly Deeply" spent two weeks at No. 1 on the *Billboard* Hot 100 and also topped the charts in Canada and Australia. The song was an even bigger adult contemporary hit, spending a jaw-dropping 11 weeks at No. 1 on the *Billboard* chart in 1998. In 2011, the publication even crowned "Truly Madly Deeply" the No. 1 Adult Contemporary single of all time.

Hayes, meanwhile, cherishes how special the song has become from an emotional standpoint. "I'm so touched 'Truly Madly Deeply' became the soundtrack to so much," he told Entertainment Focus in 2016. "Youth, first love, marriages, the '90s. There are a lot of sentimental attachments people have made to the song and I'm incredibly grateful because it was and is a very sincere personal song for me."

YOU'RE STILL THE ONE

1997 · SHANIA TWAIN

Songwriters: Robert John "Mutt" Lange and Shania Twain

SUSTAINING A MARRIAGE can be difficult. It's not just that romance can fizzle out over time—it's also that people change, priorities shift, and couples sometimes just grow apart. Shania Twain's "You're Still the One" tacitly acknowledges the challenges of making a marriage work—but, as the title implies, the country star is far more interested in toasting to a lasting, successful relationship.

Twain co-wrote "You're Still the One" with her then husband, the producer Robert John "Mutt" Lange. Although the pair would eventually divorce in 2008— and there were tabloid rumblings of marital discord even back in the 1990s— Twain told a *Boston Globe* reporter in 1997 that their marriage was solid. "We love each other in every way," she says. "We have a great creative relationship and a great personal relationship. We feel as strong as ever, and '[You're] Still the One' is sort of my own personal victory song about the marriage."

Indeed, the lyrics of "You're Still the One" possess an us-against-the-world vibe. The couple at the heart of the song say they've ignored naysayers and haters and are still madly in love—attracted to each other, affectionate, and supportive. Best of all, they're proud to have weathered any obstacles *together*—a triumph on its own.

Although Twain and Lange were working on music separately due to busy schedules, their romantic chemistry translated into studio magic. "We wrote independently and merged ideas when we joined up," Twain wrote in her autobiography, *From This Moment On*. This led to one of the song's most emotional moments: the pair affirming their love with judicious use of the title phrase. "I remember feeling very excited about the counter line sung by Mutt as backing vocals in 'You're Still the One,'" Twain said. "As I sang the chorus melody repeatedly while working out the lyrics, he kicked in with the counter line, 'You're still the one,' and it gave me chills."

"You're Still the One," which appeared on Twain's blockbuster 1997 LP, *Come on Over*, ended up as a sweeping ballad driven by thoughtful piano and a chorus bolstered by organ and twangy vocal layers. The single very quickly transcended Twain's country roots: Multiple dance remixes sprang up as B-sides, while the more earnest version of "You're Still the One" was marketed to pop and adult contemporary radio stations.

The promotion paid off. "You're Still the One" only spent one week at No. 1 on the country charts, but the single peaked at No. 2 on the *Billboard* Hot 100, becoming Twain's first top 10 crossover hit, and also topped the adult contemporary charts. In 1999, the song also won Twain two Grammy Awards, for Best Country Song and Best Female Country Vocal Performance. In ensuing years, artists such as Prince, Kelly Clarkson, Rina Sawayama, boygenius, and Tim McGraw tackled "You're the One"— while Twain herself recut the song as a duet with Elton John in 1999.

AMAZED

1999 • LONESTAR

Songwriters: Marv Green, Chris Lindsey, Aimee Mayo

THE INITIAL STAGES of romance are incomparable. You can't eat, you have trouble sleeping, you can't concentrate at work—all you can think about is when you'll be able to see (and, okay, *smooch*) your new love again. Lonestar's "Amazed" captures this intoxicating vibe to a T. In fact, the song's narrator is simply in awe of their new love—how they smell, the way they kiss, their romantic glances—and their shared physical, mental, and emotional connection. "Amazed" wants nothing more than happily ever after—and for this bond to last forever.

If "Amazed" feels very realistic, there's a good reason for it: The lyrics reflect the real-life love story of Chris Lindsey and Aimee Mayo, two of the song's three co-writers. (The other is Marv Green, a prolific songwriter with credits on hits by Tim McGraw, Reba McEntire, and Carrie Underwood.) The pair were longtime friends and frequent songwriting collaborators who ended up falling for each other as "Amazed" was coming together.

"We got together with Marv to write the song, and our feelings for each other just started coming out as we were writing," Mayo said in an interview. In a separate conversation on the *Pitch List* podcast, Lindsey concurred, adding, "We were really close, then at some point right around 'Amazed,' it all changed. When I hear that song on the radio, that's the exact feeling I had for her. That's how I felt."

"Amazed" was offered first to Boyz II Men—incredibly, the R&B group turned it down—but then landed in the laps of country band Lonestar. Sung by then vocalist Richie McDonald, the song is a soaring ballad lifted by piano, pedal steel, fiddle, and barn-burning guitars. "Amazed" spent a record eight straight weeks at No. 1 on the *Billboard* Hot Country Singles & Tracks chart.

But the song was just getting started: After being remixed for a broader music audience—among other things, this version piled on strings, and the piano and guitar became more prominent—"Amazed" then crossed over to the pop world. The tune became the first country song to reach No. 1 on the *Billboard* Hot 100 since Dolly Parton and Kenny Rogers reached the top with 1983's "Islands in the Stream" (page 93).

Perhaps because its sentiments are so timeless, "Amazed" remains just as powerful today—as evidenced by Lonestar's 2023 epic rerecording of the song with current vocalist Drew Womack. It also remains a popular song for wedding first dances—so popular that in 2009, it was even voted the No. 1 most requested song in a UK poll. "That song bottled a unique emotion to me, and I can feel that still," Lindsey has said. "I think what people feel is that."

SOMETIMES

1999 • BRITNEY SPEARS

Songwriter: Jörgen Elofsson

BRITNEY SPEARS OPTED to release a lovely ballad called "Sometimes" as the follow-up to her smash 1998 debut single, ". . . Baby One More Time." It was a canny move that positioned her as an artist with emotional depth and nuance.

"Sometimes" is a deeply relatable song about needing time and space before jumping into love. You *want* to be with someone, and trust that they have your best interests at heart, but you still think it's best to take things slow. After all, being vulnerable is still difficult and you keep sending out mixed signals—for example, pushing someone away even though you dream of being close.

During an appearance on the *Original Doll with James Rodriguez* podcast, Britney Spears's then A&R rep at Jive Records, Steve Lunt, noted that "Sometimes" originally had a different name and more mature lyrics that weren't appropriate for a teenager to sing. "I said, 'You [have] to change this up,'" Lunt said. "It's a sweet girl and a sweet song. We weren't pushing sex for Britney. That was not our plan . . . We were pushing cute. That was our thing."

The rewritten song suited Spears better—so much so that her vocal performance blew Lunt away. "As she got behind the mic, the song came to life," he shared. "It was totally different. It just had her sound . . . She brought a whole brightness to the song. She brought happiness to the song, and [soulfulness]." Musically, the song matched her hopeful vibe. Recorded at Sweden's legendary Cheiron Studios, "Sometimes" boasted a subtle R&B groove, lush keyboard layers, and a sparkling production sheen that twinkled with optimism.

In the US, "Sometimes" reached No. 21 on the pop charts and enjoyed top 40 and adult contemporary radio airplay, although the single was far more successful around the world, topping the charts in several countries and peaking at No. 3 in the UK.

THIS I PROMISE YOU

2000 • NSYNC

Songwriter: Richard Marx

IN A HEALTHY relationship, your partner serves as a buffer from life's challenging moments—the times when the world feels cruel and full of betrayal—and protects

Top 10 Unrequited-Love Songs

1. Biz Markie, "Just a Friend"
2. The Cardigans, "Lovefool"
3. Al Green, "How Can You Mend a Broken Heart"
4. Jewel, "Foolish Games"
5. Joan Jett and the Blackhearts, "I Hate Myself for Loving You"
6. Bruno Mars, "When I Was Your Man"
7. The Police, "Every Little Thing She Does Is Magic"
8. Lionel Richie, "Hello"
9. Robyn, "Dancing on My Own"
10. Rick Springfield, "Jessie's Girl"

you from hurt and pain. This is no small thing: When you feel safe and secure in a relationship, anything is possible.

Produced and written by Richard Marx, "This I Promise You" paints a picture of such a dreamlike existence. Of course, the pop hitmaker was no stranger to writing indelible love songs (see page 117 for "Right Here Waiting"), so he was a natural candidate when asked to submit a song to be considered for NSYNC's *No Strings Attached*. As luck would have it, he had started working on a song for a girl-group trio—and was able to retrofit it for the popular band. "[It] needed killer harmonies," Marx told *Entertainment Tonight*. "So, I just finished it that night with NSYNC in mind. Luckily, they loved it."

NSYNC was also the perfect group to perform "This I Promise You," because the quintet excelled at intricate, gorgeous harmonies and nailed the softhearted approach needed to make the song a success, singing each line carefully and gently as diaphanous guitars fluttered around a slow-jam groove.

In the end, Marx ultimately wished to express what everyone *hopes* happens in a successful romantic relationship. "That song certainly has lines that were personal to me," he said, "but I wanted to write one of those songs that was what everyone would love to be able to say and what everyone would love to be told."

Buoyed by that lovely aspirational vibe, "This I Promise You" resonated widely, reaching No. 5 on the *Billboard* Hot 100 and spending 13 weeks at No. 1 on *Billboard*'s Adult Contemporary chart. A Spanish language version of the song, "Yo Te Voy a Amar," was also released and appeared on *Billboard*'s Hot Latin Tracks chart in late 2000.

YOUR BODY IS A WONDERLAND

2001 • JOHN MAYER

Songwriter: John Mayer

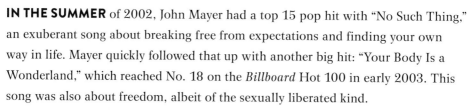

IN THE SUMMER of 2002, John Mayer had a top 15 pop hit with "No Such Thing," an exuberant song about breaking free from expectations and finding your own way in life. Mayer quickly followed that up with another big hit: "Your Body Is a Wonderland," which reached No. 18 on the *Billboard* Hot 100 in early 2003. This song was also about freedom, albeit of the sexually liberated kind.

Written from the perspective of a hopeless romantic with a carnal streak, "Your Body Is a Wonderland" is a snapshot of two people enjoying each other's company. The lyrics are full of thinly veiled innuendo—for example, references to lazing around in bed and wandering hands—but always come back to reverent worship of the physical form. Perhaps most important, Mayer's vocal delivery is earnest and sensual, not sleazy; he sounds like a Romeo treating his Juliet like a queen.

In a 2010 episode of *VH1 Storytellers*, Mayer told the real story behind "Your Body Is a Wonderland." Years before, he had moved to Atlanta and was writing songs. Among other things, he had been working up a guitar part for a while. "I would play it for hours," he recalled. "I wanted to see how liquid-y I could get it to be." That ended up becoming the beginning of "Your Body Is a Wonderland"—a syrupy, blues-inspired groove that rolled along like it was floating on a fluffy cloud. With this as a foundation, Mayer and his collaborators added various other textures—including a toy piano, a Wurlitzer electric piano, and a Hammond organ—to amplify the song's dreamlike qualities.

Over the years, people suspected "Your Body Is a Wonderland" might be about one of Mayer's high-profile girlfriends, the actress Jennifer Love Hewitt. She took the rumor in stride, telling *Entertainment Weekly* in 2007, "My body is far from a wonderland. My body is more like a pawnshop. There's a lot of interesting things put together, and if you look closely you'd probably be excited, but at first glance, not so much."

Mayer set the record straight on *VH1 Storytellers*, sharing that he wrote "Your Body Is a Wonderland" about his first girlfriend. At 14 years old, he was naturally over the moon about this love. "It was really a song about when you could love someone enough to basically jump into bed at four," he shared, "and get out of bed and it's dark."

In a late 2022 appearance on the *Call Her Daddy* podcast, Mayer reiterated this origin story but added that he preferred some mystery when talking about song meanings: "I don't like telling anyone that a song is about somebody because they're just visualizing who I'm writing about." In other words, Mayer suggests you forget the song is based on a true story—and instead let your imagination run wild.

A THOUSAND MILES

2002 • VANESSA CARLTON

Songwriter: Vanessa Carlton

PEOPLE WILL GO to great lengths to see someone they adore. Take Scottish duo the Proclaimers, who note they'll travel 500 miles to get to the house of a loved one. And then there's songwriter-pianist Vanessa Carlton, who one-ups the Proclaimers—or perhaps it's more precise to say doubles them—with her classic, "A Thousand Miles." The song discusses (what else?) how far someone would walk to see someone with whom they're smitten. Carlton pairs a waterfall-like piano riff with pirouetting strings and a yearning vocal performance—fitting, as she studied ballet very seriously—that combine for an innocent, dreamlike song.

Carlton initially wrote the song's piano riff at age 17, on a Yamaha upright piano in her parents' sunroom. "The song is about a crush I had on a Juilliard student," she recalled in a 2021 *Vice* documentary, declining to name the person because they ended up becoming a well-known actor. "I would never talk to this person; I was very shy. I was like, 'There's just no way in God's creation that this would ever happen.'" Other lyrics referenced New York City, where Carlton had moved to study ballet, and hinted at the luxurious freedom of being a carefree young adult living in a big city.

Incredibly, "A Thousand Miles" wasn't the song's original title. At first, Carlton insisted that the song should be called "Interlude." Her future record label balked at the name—"I had to say, 'Look, I'm the president of the label, we're not calling it "Interlude,"'" then A&M Records head Ron Fair told MTV News—

as did other labels. "I'll never forget people's suggestions for other titles," Carlton said in the same article. "Another label wanted me to name it 'Downtown Tonight.' Needless to say, I didn't sign with them."

Fair loved the demo of "A Thousand Miles" despite the song's name and worked with Carlton to perfect the arrangement and execution. The work paid off: The lead single from Carlton's debut album, *Be Not Nobody*, "A Thousand Miles" spent seven weeks at No. 1 on *Billboard*'s Adult Contemporary chart and reached No. 5 on the Hot 100—leading to nominations for Record of the Year and Song of the Year at the Grammys. It's also been covered by the cast of *Glee*, as well as Christian Lee Hutson, Victoria Justice, David Archuleta, and others.

And, today, people are still trying to use new methods of transportation to reach their crush. In 2023, a 34-year-old aerospace engineer named Ben Howard re-created the song's iconic music video—which found Carlton being filmed playing her piano while traveling around a city—in San Francisco, albeit this time starring a robotic puppet designed to look like the musician.

ALL THE THINGS SHE SAID

2002 · T.A.T.U.

Songwriters: Sergio Galoyan, Trevor Horn, Martin Kierszenbaum, Elena Kiper, Valery Polienko

QUEER ARTISTS—AND songs about queer love and desire—have a prominent place in modern pop music. But t.A.T.u.'s "All the Things She Said"—a song written from the perspective of a woman harboring strong romantic feelings for another

woman—was an outlier upon its 2002 release. The song's narrator can't stop thinking about her crush and their conversations and refuses to feel ashamed of her desires. She hopes one day they can be together, away from people who think the couple is a curiosity.

Cocreated by Ivan Shapovalov, t.A.T.u. was a Russian duo featuring two teenagers, Julia Volkova and Lena Katina. The group issued a successful Russian-language debut album in 2001, *200 Po Vstrechnoy*, that featured songs like "Ya Soshla S Uma," the Russian version of what would later become "All the Things She Said."

According to lore, this song came about after co-writer Elena Kiper went to the dentist and was medicated for a procedure—and dreamed that she kissed another woman. "She woke up saying, 'I've lost my mind!'" journalist Daisy Jones told NPR. "And that refrain was going around and around in her mind for a while after this dental surgery."

When it came time to shape t.A.T.u.'s songs for American audiences, for an album called *200 km/h in the Wrong Lane*, Interscope Records hired musician/producer Trevor Horn for the job. Horn was no stranger to making hits: A member of synth-pop act the Buggles, he cofounded ZTT Records—which had massive success with Frankie Goes to Hollywood—and produced hit albums for Yes, ABC, and Seal.

Working up English-language versions of t.A.T.u.'s songs proved to be quite a challenge. "Interestingly enough, I thought when they offered it to me, I thought I was gonna get the multitrack from the Russian version but they wouldn't give it to me, so I had to completely remake the record," Horn told the *Guardian*. That included putting together a translation of the lyrics—and identifying elements that made the song successful in Russian, such as repeating several phrases—working on vocals, and even re-creating the music: sleek Europop with nods to circa-Y2K techno and trance ambience.

"There was no budget, so I had to play all the instruments myself," Horn said. "My late wife said, 'You had all these bloody guitars, time to put them to use!' I ended up quite enjoying it really. Sometimes records come out well, sometimes they don't, but that one did."

Indeed, "All the Things She Said" reached No. 20 on the *Billboard* Hot 100 and topped the charts around the world, and *200 km/h in the Wrong Lane* also became a sales success. Stylistically, the group's dance-friendly, sugary synth-pop sound would soon come to dominate the 2000s. And although "All the Things She Said" is still considered a milestone for queer pop, t.A.T.u.'s legacy is more complex. As it turns out, neither member of the band identified as queer at the time they released the song—and years later, Volkova drew intense backlash for making homophobic comments.

CRAZY IN LOVE

2003 · BEYONCÉ

Songwriters: Rich Harrison, Jay-Z, Beyoncé Knowles, Eugene Record

IN THE LATE 1990s and early 2000s, Beyoncé enjoyed plenty of commercial success with Destiny's Child. When she prepared to release her debut solo album, 2003's *Dangerously in Love*, she made a big splash with the record's first single, "Crazy in Love."

Bold and brassy, the strutting tune is built around an upbeat sample plucked from the Chi-Lites' "Are You My Woman? (Tell Me So)" and a relentless dance groove. (The Chi-Lites' Eugene Record received a songwriting credit for the sample.) Beyoncé sounds extra confident in the spotlight, between her stuttering "oh-oh-oh" parts and her lightning-fast delivery on the verses, as she talks about how much a romantic partner drives her wild. "Crazy in Love" might have been built from classic parts—but it felt fresh and new.

Top 10 Relationship Revenge Songs

1. Beyoncé, "Sorry"
2. The Chicks, "Goodbye Earl"
3. Kelly Clarkson, "Since U Been Gone"
4. Fleetwood Mac, "Silver Springs"
5. Reba McEntire, "The Night the Lights Went Out in Georgia"
6. Alanis Morissette, "You Oughta Know"
7. Carly Simon, "You're So Vain"
8. Nancy Sinatra, "These Boots Are Made for Walkin'"
9. Taylor Swift, "Picture to Burn"
10. Carrie Underwood, "Before He Cheats"

In an MTV interview, Beyoncé credited the "horn hook" for making "Crazy in Love" such an irresistible song. "It has this go-go feel to it, this old-school feel. I wasn't sure if people were going to get it." Producer Rich Harrison, who had earmarked the Chi-Lites song for a track, also knew it could be a tough sell, he told MTV.

But Beyoncé liked the sample and thought it had potential—so much so that she reportedly instructed Harrison to come up with a song around the horns in just two hours. It was a big lift, especially since the producer happened to be hungover from a night of partying, but he succeeded in sketching out the meat of the song.

As it turns out, the title ended up having somewhat of a double meaning. While in the studio, Beyoncé wanted to take a break and buy her Destiny's Child bandmate Kelly Rowland a birthday present but was reluctant to leave due to the potential for paparazzi. "[In the studio] I was looking crazy with my clothes,"

Beyoncé told *The Guardian*, noting that she was wearing a mismatched outfit and had messy hair. "And I kept saying, 'I'm looking crazy right now.'" A lightbulb went off for Harrison—that was the hook!

Her then boyfriend (now husband) Jay-Z later added his part, a memorable rap full of swagger that illustrates why he's hip-hop royalty. "I remember when I first heard Jay's version," Harrison recalled to MTV. "I was in my car screaming, 'Whoaaaa!'"

Listeners had the same reaction. "Crazy in Love" won two Grammy Awards for Best R&B Song and Best Rap/Sung Collaboration and reached No. 1 on the pop, dance, and R&B/hip-hop *Billboard* charts. It also set Beyoncé up for a thriving solo career that's still gaining creative momentum more than two decades later.

YOU RAISE ME UP

2003 · JOSH GROBAN

Songwriters: Rolf Løvland (music); Brendan Graham (lyrics)

"YOU RAISE ME UP" is a perfect example of a love song that means different things to different people—and it might not even be perceived as a love song at all. At its core, the song is about drawing strength and support from someone else. Because of them, you can do seemingly impossible things—for example, traverse dangerous waters and perch atop a mountain—and are emotionally equipped to handle life's big obstacles.

Now, this *seems* to describe a solid romantic partnership. But some people see it as a song about religious faith—where a higher power is the one providing this guidance and care—while others play the song at funerals, as they see the lyrics as a comforting sign from a dearly departed loved one. None of these interpretations are wrong—if anything, they all speak to the restorative power of feeling cared for and loved.

As it happens, the last interpretation holds some weight, as "You Raise Me Up" was first played at the funeral of co-writer Rolf Løvland's mother. Moreover, the first version of the song, heard on 2002's *Once in a Red Moon* by Løvland's group, Secret Garden, is quite somber. Sung by the Irish musician Brian Kennedy, the tune incorporates Celtic folk flourishes such as uilleann pipes and a tin whistle, and contributions from the London Community Gospel Choir and the Irish choral group ANÚNA. The lovely lyrics, meanwhile, are courtesy of Brendan Graham, an author and songwriter who wrote the Eurovision Song Contest–winning tunes "Rock 'n' Roll Kids" and "The Voice."

Although dozens of artists have covered "You Raise Me Up," the most recognizable version is by Josh Groban. Released on his second album, 2003's *Closer*, and produced by David Foster, it maintains the solemn vibe of the original, thanks to elegiac piano, stately strings, and Groban's magisterial vocals. But there's a distinctly uplifting vibe to this take, thanks in no small part to the gospel choir that chimes in during the latter part of the song, bringing spiritual tranquility to an already lovely song.

Groban's version spent six weeks atop *Billboard*'s Adult Contemporary chart in 2004 and crossed over to the pop charts, reaching No. 76, in addition to being nominated for a Grammy for Best Male Pop Vocal Performance. Over the years, he also performed the song at multiple high-profile events, such as Oprah Winfrey's festive 50th-birthday bash and at the Super Bowl to honor the crew lost in the 2003 space shuttle *Columbia* explosion. Once again, "You Raise Me Up" could be used to celebrate happiness—or honor important people we've lost.

IF I AIN'T GOT YOU

2003 • ALICIA KEYS

Songwriter: Alicia Keys

ALICIA KEYS'S "If I Ain't Got You" is a pointed reminder of something very important: When push comes to shove, a relationship isn't defined by owning fancy baubles, receiving gorgeous roses, or achieving fame and fortune—it's about being with the person you love. In fact, these expensive things are meaningless if you don't have someone with whom to share them.

Written and produced by Keys, "If I Ain't Got You" sadly arose out of a terrible tragedy: the 2001 plane crash death of the promising R&B star Aaliyah. "The song idea came together right after Aaliyah passed away," Keys said (as quoted by *Complex*). "It was such a sad time and no one wanted to believe it. It just made everything crystal clear to me—what matters, and what doesn't." Coincidentally, Keys was on a plane herself not long after the crash, a situation that magnified her feelings. "There was just this sentiment of being present in the moment," she later said in an interview for the TV show *The Voice*, on which she was a judge, "and really nothing else mattering but those that you love."

Fittingly, "If I Ain't Got You" is a relatively simple song driven by minimalist beats, jazzy piano, and fuzz-coated horns. "I wrote it really quickly, but in order to produce it the way that you hear it, it took forever," Keys later said. "Nothing would come out right. Every version that I did, every arrangement that I did was just wrong. It was such a labor of love." Despite all the work she put into it, Keys almost gave the song to Christina Aguilera to record; unsurprisingly, Keys said in a 2020 interview that her record label was aghast at the thought.

Keeping "If I Ain't Got You" for herself turned out to be a wise move. A highlight of 2003's *The Diary of Alicia Keys*, the song reached No. 4 on the *Billboard* Hot 100 and spent six weeks at No. 1 on the Hot R&B/Hip-Hop Singles chart. Keys also won a Grammy for Best Female R&B Vocal Performance for "If I Ain't Got You," although the song lost in the prestigious Song of the Year category.

Multiple artists have covered "If I Ain't Got You," and the song has become an inspirational touchstone; for example, British swimmer Kelly Holmes used the song as motivation as she won two gold medals at the 2004 Summer Olympics. Keys herself always treats the song with reverence. In 2023, she recorded a new version of the song for the Netflix series *Queen Charlotte: A Bridgerton Story.* The tune features a 74-piece orchestra comprising women of color and conducted by Ofentse Pitse, the first South African woman to lead an all-Black orchestra. The moving video for this version received an MTV Video Music Award nomination.

MAPS

2003 • YEAH YEAH YEAHS

Songwriters: Brian Chase, Karen O, Nick Zinner

WHEN IT COMES to indie rock love songs, the New York City trio Yeah Yeah Yeahs set the blueprint with "Maps." Piercing guitar shivers and geometric drum patterns bolster a deeply vulnerable performance from the band's vocalist, Karen O. Although known for an over-the-top stage presence, she sounds subdued and dispirited on "Maps."

"There's a lot of loooove in that song," Karen O told *Rolling Stone*. "But there's a lot of fear, too. I exposed myself so much with that song, I kind of shocked myself." That's because of the subject matter: In "Maps," she was singing about her ex-boyfriend, Angus Andrew, who fronted a rhythm-heavy rock band called Liars. In the lyrics, she pleads for him to stay—and stay with her—as she stresses the couple are two of a kind. The insinuation is that he's leaving on tour (hence the references to maps), although the song also works on a more metaphorical level: She fears he might be experiencing wanderlust and she wants to reassure him that the familiar (and close to home) are just as special.

"Maps" is also known for a touching music video, during which Karen O starts crying—a real response, she later said, as Andrew was three hours late to the video shoot. "I was just about to leave for tour," she told Contact Music. "I didn't think he was even going to come, and this was the song that was written for him. He eventually showed up and I got myself in a real emotional state."

Over the years, "Maps" has crossed over into some unexpected places, starting with mainstream pop music. As legend has it, Kelly Clarkson's barn-burning "Since U Been Gone" emerged after the writing team of Max Martin and Dr. Luke was dissecting "Maps." (Fittingly, the musician Ted Leo underscored the similarities with a live cover that mashed up both songs.)

"I said, 'Ah, I love this song,' and Max was like, 'If they would just write a damn pop chorus on it!'" Dr. Luke told *Billboard*. "It was driving him nuts, because that indie song was sort of on six, going to seven, going to eight, the chorus comes . . . and it goes back down to five. It drove him crazy. And when he said that, it was like, lightbulb. 'Why don't we do that, but put a big chorus on it?' It worked."

The tune also struck a deep chord with the Yeah Yeah Yeahs' peers, as both the White Stripes and Arcade Fire covered the song. Years later, Anderson .Paak and the

Bad Plus put their own spin on the song, while Beyoncé also interpolated a line from "Maps" on her *Lemonade* song "Hold Up." In 2021, the tune also landed at No. 101 on *Rolling Stone*'s list of the 500 Greatest Songs of All Time.

I WILL FOLLOW
YOU INTO THE DARK

2005 • DEATH CAB FOR CUTIE

Songwriter: Ben Gibbard

IN THE EARLY 2000s, the Bellingham, Washington, band Death Cab for Cutie became known as the patron saints of emotional anguish. Their songs touched on relatable relationship problems—for example, 2003's *Transatlanticism* chronicled the unique angst of long-distance romance—and nailed the complexities of navigating adulthood.

In 2005, Death Cab for Cutie released one of its most straightforward and haunting songs, "I Will Follow You into the Dark." Driven by simple acoustic guitar and Ben Gibbard's doleful vocals, the tune proposes a morbid but comforting thought: If and when your partner dies, you'll have no problem accompanying them into the afterlife. Of course, the song isn't exactly sure what comes with death—heaven and hell might be full, for example—and it's possible that your beloved won't need a companion. But the narrator is in the relationship for the proverbial long haul—whatever that means.

As with many Death Cab for Cutie songs, the idea grew out of things Gibbard was thinking about and experiencing in his own life. "I'm also at an age now where it's like, all of a sudden, I'm thinking about larger concepts that are really freaking me out," Gibbard told *Chord* magazine. "Like the idea of death, and what happens to us after we die, and being in a situation where I'm with somebody who I really care about, and I realize the weight of these relationships."

The titular phrase popped into Gibbard's head one day while the musician was commuting to the makeshift studio he had put together in a downtown Seattle apartment. Once he arrived, he grabbed an acoustic guitar and the song poured out of him "very quickly, in like 15 or 20 minutes," he told *NME* in 2018. "It was as if the song was being beamed down to me," he said. "I wasn't necessarily writing it as much as I was channeling it."

Recording the song was just as spontaneous. While Death Cab for Cutie was in the studio recording their 2005 album, *Plans*, the session paused to address a headphone mix issue. Gibbard idly picked up his guitar and started playing "I Will Follow You into The Dark," which the band had planned on recording later. The sparse sound intrigued guitarist/producer Chris Walla.

"[Ben] was still coming through the vocal mic as he was playing this, and it was sounding really cool to me, so I went up and said, 'Let's track this real quick,' and we did," he told *Mix*. "That's what's on the record. It was a mono recording with no effects."

Of course, "I Will Follow You into The Dark" isn't exactly the cheeriest love song ever, Gibbard noted. But the song's sonic rawness no doubt has much to do with its appeal—as does Gibbard's willingness to talk about taboo topics like death and the promise of eternal fidelity. "We like to think that when people leave this life, we will see them again someday," he told *NME*. "Writing a love song that deals specifically with the inevitable death of one's partner—and that you will follow that person into whatever the afterlife is or is not—that's something that people can relate to."

MAKE YOU FEEL MY LOVE

2008 •ADELE

Songwriter: Bob Dylan

ADELE ISN'T JUST a once-in-a-lifetime vocalist. She's also a masterful interpreter of other people's works. For example, her version of the Cure's "Lovesong" is sparse and affecting, with a bossa nova beat that adds nostalgic melancholy. Similarly, her 2008 ballad version of Bob Dylan's "Make You Feel My Love" is relatively unadorned, driven by just minimalist piano, and captures the guttural ache of pining after someone. "The lyrics are just amazing and summed up exactly what I'd been trying to say in my songs," Adele told the *Yorkshire Post*. "It's about regretting not being with someone, and it's beautiful." It was also quite successful, reaching No. 4 on the UK charts in 2010.

Of course, Adele is far from the only artist to cover "Make You Feel My Love." It's considered a modern standard, a tune tackled by Pink, Garth Brooks, Bryan Ferry, Engelbert Humperdinck (duetting with Willie Nelson), Billy Joel, Neil Diamond, and Kelly Clarkson. But the meaning of "Make You Feel My Love" isn't necessarily obviously about regret or lost love.

That's not a surprise given who wrote it: the notoriously slippery Bob Dylan. "Make You Feel My Love" originally appeared on Dylan's Grammy-winning 1997 album, *Time Out of Mind,* and "arrived as a latecomer" during the album sessions, producer Daniel Lanois told *The Guardian*. "It was a surprise—but we like surprises." Like the Adele version, it was also quite simple, dominated by organ, piano, and Dylan's trademark raconteur-like intoning, Lanois noted. "It was pretty much straight off the floor—live vocal—and a nice reminder that a spontaneous moment can be captured that way."

Lyrically, "Make You Feel My Love" also feels freewheeling and vulnerable, with a narrator ticking off the things they would do to woo their beloved—shielding them from inclement weather, providing physical solace, forgoing food and creature comforts, and treating them well. "People like romantic songs, don't they?" Lanois told *The Guardian*. "It's a very deep, romantic song. It's nice to hear Bob deliver such a sentiment."

But Don Was, who produced Brooks's version for the 1998 film *Hope Floats*, points out something interesting: Listeners might interpret "Make You Feel My Love" as a successful love song—but there's no guarantee the cajoling will work. "Does he believe he's going to get the girl, or doesn't he?" Was told *The Guardian*. "You suspect he doesn't . . . [But] Bob did this in his vocal—he walked the line. He never gave away whether he felt defeated or optimistic. That's the suspense of the song."

Adele too has broadened her interpretation of the song, dedicating it to the rapper Stormzy in 2016 and even serenading a newly engaged couple with the song during a 2021 concert at Los Angeles's Griffith Observatory. Where "Make You Feel My Love" is concerned, it's a thin line between love—and everything else.

LOVE STORY

2008 • TAYLOR SWIFT

Songwriter: Taylor Swift

TAYLOR SWIFT'S MONUMENTAL Eras Tour concerts contained countless memorable moments: a career-spanning setlist, surprise acoustic songs, and duets with Phoebe Bridgers, Jack Antonoff, HAIM, and the National's Aaron Dessner. For many couples, however, Swift's nightly performance of the *Fearless* highlight "Love Story" provided an opportunity for more intimate memories.

The hit—which reimagines the tragic tale of Shakespeare's Romeo and Juliet with a happy ending—includes the perfect backdrop for an engagement: an epic key change leading into a lyric about Romeo proposing to Juliet. Multiple videos of in-concert proposals indeed surfaced and went viral; inevitably, these clips featured couples embracing, kissing, and crying at this very moment in the song.

"Love Story" is truly romantic first and foremost because of the lyrics. Swift wrote the song from the perspective of Juliet, a spunky and optimistic daydreamer who falls head over heels for Romeo over the objection of her parents. Although she frets that her beau is going to ghost her, he comes through in the end with an engagement ring *and* the approval of Juliet's dad.

In a 2009 interview with *Time*, Swift said she wrote "Love Story" on her bedroom floor "in about 20 minutes," basing it on a true story that wasn't quite so cheery: Her friends and family immediately disliked a guy she wanted to date. "All of them!" she said. "For the first time, I could relate to that Romeo-and-Juliet situation where the only people who wanted them to be together were them. That's the most romantic song I've written, and it's not even about a person I really dated."

Swift recorded "Love Story" at Nashville's Blackbird Studio, co-producing the song with Nathan Chapman. To maximize the tune's impact, she released "Love Story" in a pop and country version. The latter had an old-fashioned feel, thanks to keening fiddle, easygoing banjo, and ornate mandolin, while the pop version emphasized soft-glow beats and insistent electric guitars. Both takes, however, boasted a keen sense of dynamics, meaning that the song reaches an ecstatic peak right at the moment where Swift reveals the engagement of Romeo and Juliet.

Having the different versions ended up being a

smart strategy, as "Love Story" reached No. 1 on two *Billboard* radio airplay charts, in pop and country—the first song ever to achieve this feat. Overall, the song was also Swift's highest-charting pop song at the time; it peaked at No. 4 on the *Billboard* Hot 100.

Much like the Shakespeare tale on which it was based, "Love Story" has had remarkable staying power. In 2021, Swift released a rerecorded version of the song called "Love Story (Taylor's Version)" that lovingly re-created the original's classic country vibe. Like that take, this new version reached No. 1 on *Billboard*'s Hot Country Songs chart—making Swift the only artist besides Dolly Parton to top the chart with a single *and* its rerecorded version. In another nod to the song's enduring popularity, "Love Story (Taylor's Version)" won the first-ever Trending Comeback Song of the Year at the 2022 CMT Music Awards. As it turns out, nobody can resist a satisfying romantic ending—especially when it leads to happily ever after.

LOVE IN THIS CLUB

2008 • USHER FEATURING YOUNG JEEZY

Songwriters: Usher Raymond, Polow da Don, Young Jeezy, Lamar Taylor, Ryon Lovett, Keith Thomas, Darnell Dalton

SOMETIMES LOVE BEGINS over a romantic candlelight dinner in a fancy restaurant. At other times, sparks fly in a nightclub amid thumping beats and bottle service. And on more debauched nights, a couple might skip the getting-to-know you part altogether and decide to get busy in a bathroom.

As it happens, Usher describes the latter scenario in his No. 1 single "Love in This Club." The song is a laid-back R&B ballad with silk-bedsheet grooves and pulsating beats. Despite its potential for raunchiness, "Love in This Club" instead comes across as sexy squarely because of Usher, who combines a come-hither delivery with his signature seductive croon. Even if a steamy club hookup *doesn't* happen, Usher makes sure the song conveys a realistic fantasy.

As producer Polow da Don told MTV News, "Love in This Club" isn't necessarily meant to show any romantic consummation. "The song is not really all about having sex in the club, it's about having that urge," he said. "It's about meeting somebody for the first time, and you kinda wish nobody was there. You're like, 'You're the one.' Lust at first sight."

That being said, the producer modeled his music after one of the biggest party cities in the world, Las Vegas, following a fun-filled weekend in Sin City. "If you listen to the beat, the synths and everything has a Vegas feel to it," Polow da Don said. "Making love in the club, people in Vegas are kinda wild. Vegas had that 'I don't care, I'm living life' attitude."

At the time the song was released, Usher had settled down a bit and gotten married. "After all of the talk about my relationship, I wouldn't come out with a song about my relationship, because you already know about that," he told *Entertainment Weekly.* "And I'm never gonna make love in a club with a girl."

The song's featured guest, Young Jeezy, told MTV News that rapping about getting busy in a club was also out of character for him, so he also stuck to what he knew best. "I just did me on the song," he said. "I don't get a chance to talk to the ladies a lot. If I had a chance to talk to them, that's what I would say: 'I'm what you want; I'm what you need.'"

"Love in This Club," which appeared on Usher's 2008 album, *Here I Stand,* spent three weeks atop the *Billboard* Hot 100 and had a four-week run at No. 1 on *Billboard*'s Hot R&B/Hip-Hop Songs chart. Not content with this success, Usher released a remix of the song, "Love in This Club, Pt. II," as the album's second single.

This redo boasted a throwback '90s R&B slow jam vibe and even more personality thanks to guest appearances from Beyoncé and Lil Wayne. "Love in This Club, Pt. II" was also a huge crossover hit, reaching No. 18 on the Billboard Hot 100 and the top 10 of *Billboard*'s Hot R&B/Hip-Hop Songs chart.

HOME

2009 • EDWARD SHARPE AND THE MAGNETIC ZEROS

Songwriters: Jade Castrinos and Alex Ebert

EVEN IF YOU think you're *not* familiar with Edward Sharpe and the Magnetic Zeros' "Home"—a cheerful folk-rock tune that sounds like something you'd hear during a campfire sing-along—chances are good you've heard the song before. It's been used in multiple TV shows (including *Glee* and *Community*) and in advertisements around the world, while a lilting cover by a fictional artist named Edith Whiskers went viral in recent years and remains omnipresent in videos.

"Home" is also far and away the biggest hit for Edward Sharpe and the Magnetic Zeros. The band name is somewhat misleading: Edward Sharpe wasn't a real person but the alter ego of group leader Alex Ebert. The transformation is impressive, as Ebert was previously the front man of early-2000s synth-pop revivalists Ima Robot. "I do feel like I had lost my identity in general," he told San Diego News Network in 2009. "I really didn't know what was going on or who I was anymore. Adopting another name helped me open up an avenue to get back."

The idea of finding a place where you feel most like yourself—and a place where you belong—certainly permeates "Home." But in the song, this place is with a person: Ebert and his then girlfriend Jade Castrinos co-wrote the whirlwind tune about their own love story. Together, they pepper the lyrics with lighthearted rhymes and a reference to a fateful night when a nasty fall led to a hospital visit and the realization that love was in the air. "Home" resembles a childlike nursery rhyme full of innocence; at one point, Ebert even namechecks a few things—pumpkin pie, candy, Jesus—that aren't as great as his beloved.

Sadly, the idyllic romance described in "Home" didn't last; Ebert and Castrinos eventually broke up, and she and the group parted ways in 2014. That same year, Ebert won a Golden Globe for Best Original Score for his work on the Robert Redford film *All Is Lost*—and he now primarily focuses on writing and spiritual endeavors.

THE ONLY EXCEPTION

2009 • PARAMORE

Songwriters: Josh Farro and Hayley Williams

PARAMORE IS KNOWN as one of the most galvanizing rock bands around, thanks in no small part to Hayley Williams. The fiery figurehead commands the stage with confident dance moves and an even bolder voice. But Paramore has never been afraid to be vulnerable—as evidenced by "The Only Exception," found on the 2009 album *Brand New Eyes*. Co-written by Williams and guitarist Josh Farro, the exquisite ballad was much different from other Paramore songs to date: Driven by fluttering acoustic guitars, soft-glow organ, and subtle vocal shading, the song shines due to its delicate nuances.

Paramore didn't have any concerns about going in a softer direction, however. In fact, Williams was blown away by Farro's music. "I thought it was so beautiful," she told *Kerrang!* "I don't know where my head was at when I heard it, but it really hit me." Williams first considered making the song into a shorter, stripped-down piece but decided that the full-band treatment was best after she wrote the lyrics.

"The Only Exception" starts with Williams delving into some painful memories from her own life—derived from her parents' contentious marriage and tumultuous relationship to love—and vowing she wouldn't sing about love if she didn't mean it. "The first verse is about where I think the fear to be open or vulnerable started," she told *Kerrang!*, adding that her own family's tumult is well known. "It's something that's kinda stayed with me and I've learned from."

Accordingly, in the next verse of the song, Williams describes how growing up in this kind of environment made her wary of opening her heart or giving in to love. Instead, she chose loneliness because it was safer. Then we find out what the chorus means: Williams has finally found someone worth loving—they're "the only exception" to her previously hard-line rules.

As it happens, Williams soon realized "The Only Exception" was her very first love song. "Even if I've tried in the past, this is the first one that I'm really proud of," she told *Alternative Press* in 2010. "I like that I was able to express the fact that I have always been really afraid of love—and I still am at times—but the excitement and the hope that it exists is still very evident in the lyrics. So it's not like I'm a total cynic!"

The song's lonely-to-loved story resonated deeply with fans, and the song became a big hit for Paramore, reaching No. 24 on the *Billboard* Hot 100.

JUST THE WAY YOU ARE

2010 • BRUNO MARS

Songwriters: Khari Cain, Philip Lawrence,
Ari Levine, Bruno Mars, Khalil Walton

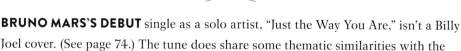

BRUNO MARS'S DEBUT single as a solo artist, "Just the Way You Are," isn't a Billy Joel cover. (See page 74.) The tune does share some thematic similarities with the Piano Man's hit—among other things, telling a lady that she's perfect the way she is and doesn't need to change a thing about herself. But Bruno Mars's lyrics have more of a reassuring vibe, as the woman at the song's center is insecure about her looks. In fact, the song gets specific about her beautiful features—her smile, her lips, her eyes—to emphasize this beauty.

"You know, there's no mind-boggling lyrics or twists in the story—they just come directly from the heart," he told *Blues & Soul*. "There's nothing mind-blowing about it. I'm just telling a woman she looks beautiful the way she is—and, let's be honest, what woman doesn't wanna hear those lyrics?"

Mars was no stranger to hitmaking when he released "Just the Way You Are." He had already co-written songs for Cobra Starship ("Hot Mess"), Matisyahu ("One Day"), and Flo Rida ("Right Round"). He also contributed guest vocals on several big hits (B.o.B's "Nothin' on You," Travie McCoy's "Billionaire"). All of that work had an effect on "Just the Way You Are," he told the *Los Angeles Times*: "Writing for other artists helped me figure out that magic you have to capture to make everyone connect with a song."

Of course, it helped that Mars co-produced and co-wrote "Just the Way You Are" with Phil Lawrence and Ari Levine, his collaborators in production squad the Smeczingtons. Plus, the trio was able to work off a piece of music penned by co-producer Needlz that was intended for rapper Lupe Fiasco—until Mars sang the hook and ended up using it himself.

Mars added he also took inspiration from tunes "that stand the test of time" while writing the song, particularly Eric Clapton's "Wonderful Tonight" and Sinéad O'Connor's "Nothing Compares 2 U." Both of those songs have opposing themes— Clapton's song is about adoring someone beautiful, while O'Connor's take is a wrenching breakup tune—but each composition is well crafted and uses classic instrumentation. "Just the Way You Are" employs bouncy piano and a rhythmic foundation indebted to jazz-inflected '90s hip-hop—a perfect match for Mars's earnest vocal delivery and old-school vibe.

"Just the Way You Are" was a global smash, reaching No. 1 in the US, UK, Canada, and Australia, among other places. It was also nominated for a Grammy for Best Pop Vocal Performance. The single also set Mars up for a decorated career as a solo artist and collaborator in groups such as the luxurious funk-rock band Silk Sonic.

TEENAGE DREAM

2010 • KATY PERRY

Songwriters: Lukasz Gottwald, Benjamin Levin,
Bonnie McKee, Max Martin, Katy Perry

LOVE JUST SOMEHOW feels different when you're a teenager—more colorful and more exhilarating. That's partly because you might be experiencing many things for the first time: first stomach butterflies, first dates, first kisses, first make-out sessions. But the future also seems wide open with teenage love—anything can and *does* happen.

That's very much the vibe of Katy Perry's "Teenage Dream." The song captures a sky's-the-limit vibe of a teenage romance: making yourself vulnerable for the first time, going on an adventure that involves beach drinking and making a fort in a hotel, and embracing the feeling that you'll be together forever.

Best of all, "Teenage Dream" emphasizes the joy of finding someone who accepts you for who you are. Add in some flirtatious references to tight jeans and sexual dalliances—and a synth-driven arrangement that wouldn't have felt out of place in the top 40 during the 1980s—and it's a fizzy recipe for a red-hot romance.

Perry and co-writer Bonnie McKee "wrote and rewrote this song four times," the latter said in a 2010 interview. "It started off being kind of a 'forever young' idea. That was always the spirit of it. Katy started with a lyric about Peter Pan that was cool, but it just kept feeling too young, and we wanted it to have more edge, more sex." McKee adds that the duo landed on a concept along those lines, "comparing the feeling of wearing new clothes to sex," but the idea was turned down.

Undeterred, McKee dug up memories of being a teenager—which for her involved slumber parties full of boy-crazy discussions, viewings of Baz Luhrmann's *Romeo + Juliet*, and crushing on '90s heartthrob Leonardo DiCaprio—and developed new lyrical angles. Unfortunately, during a subsequent recording session with producers Lukasz Gottwald (aka Dr. Luke) and Max Martin, she was initially deterred from sharing her concept for the chorus. Luckily, however, she spoke up at the last minute, after Perry had recorded the song. "I pulled Luke and Max aside and told them about my idea," McKee said. "When I sang it to them, they said, 'Well why didn't you say that in the first place?!'"

The switch ended up being for the best. "Teenage Dream" spent two weeks at No. 1 on the *Billboard* Hot 100 and was also nominated for a Grammy Award for Best Female Pop Vocal Performance. The song has also become one of Perry's signature tunes—an ode to young love that never gets old.

WE FOUND LOVE

2011 • RIHANNA

Songwriter: Calvin Harris

RIHANNA WAS ALREADY a massive global superstar upon the release of her 2011 album, *Talk That Talk*, thanks to previous hit songs such as "Umbrella" and "Only Girl (In the World)." But with the launch of "We Found Love"—the first single from *Talk That Talk*—she soared into elite pop stratospheres. Teaming up with Scottish producer-songwriter-DJ Calvin Harris, Rihanna unleashed a note-perfect EDM anthem rooted in ecstatic electro house and techno.

Atop surging beats and massive beat drops, and with desperation seeping into her voice, she expresses a very relatable experience: getting into a sticky romantic entanglement. Maybe it's falling for someone when the odds seem stacked against you, getting into an unhealthy relationship, or becoming involved with someone who might not be good for you. In other words, there are pros *and* cons to the relationship—and it's unclear whether the good outweighs the bad. "It makes you feel so good, like you're lost in electricity or love or whatever it is," Melina Matsoukas, who directed the song's music video, told MTV News.

Interestingly enough, Harris originally recorded "We Found Love" with someone else, the British R&B/soul singer Leona Lewis. But the Rihanna version was chosen instead, Lewis told *NME*, ostensibly after Harris toured with Rihanna. "I didn't commit to it because I wanted 'Trouble' to be my first single, so I think that was another reason they went with Rihanna." This switch wasn't necessarily out of the ordinary, Lewis added: "There are so many songs I've recorded, only to hear other people singing them. It happens all the time. It was a bit annoying to see how big a hit it was around the world, but if I'd released it maybe it wouldn't have done as well."

"We Found Love" indeed became a monstrous worldwide hit, reaching No. 1 in nearly 30 countries—including the US, where it spent 10 weeks atop the *Billboard* Hot 100. As of 2023, it was Rihanna's longest-running chart-topping single in America. For good measure, the song's music video—which depicted both the good and bad parts of a relationship—picked up a Grammy for Best Short Form Music Video.

"[The song's] totally rave-y . . . and that's the feeling, just music rushing over you, and then I started thinking about drugs and addiction and love and how that's an addiction," Matsoukas told MTV News. "We've all lived the ups and downs of being in a toxic relationship. It's really about the obstacles of trying to let it go, but at the same time how great it makes you feel, so it's hard to let it go."

I CHOOSE YOU

2013 • SARA BAREILLES

Songwriters: Sara Bareilles, Jason Blynn, Pete Harper

SARA BAREILLES ISN'T necessarily the first person you think of when the topic of love songs comes up. That might seem like an odd statement, considering that she titled her debut single "Love Song"—and this jaunty tune became a massive hit that reached No. 4 on the *Billboard* Hot 100 and received two Grammy nominations. But "Love Song" is actually a misnomer: In reality, Bareilles wrote the song about the fact that she *wouldn't* write a love song to please her record label.

Still, Bareilles isn't averse to love. That was evident on "I Choose You," an ornate chamber-pop number punctuated by bass, cello, piano, and guitar. The song reads like wedding vows: The lyrics mention sharing hearts forever and coming together as a pair, while the narrator admits they weren't sure they'd ever find love.

Being with their beloved also helps them weather proverbial (and actual) storms. What's most poignant is the title: The narrator is actively deciding to be with their significant other—a telling declaration of love and fidelity.

Bareilles told Pride Source that "I Choose You" came from a "backhanded compliment" she received from a fan. "The song was inspired by a guy who came up to me after a show and said, 'My wife and I wanted to use your music in our wedding, but everything you write is so depressing.' I thought about my catalog of songs, and went, 'Wow, I haven't really said anything positive about love yet.'"

The music video for "I Choose You" underscored the song's message. The clip goes behind the scenes as Bareilles helps orchestrate the marriage proposals of two couples: Los Angeles residents Matt and Chelsea, and a Denver couple named Aly and Andrea. (Bareilles later shared that Aly and Andrea "were so courageous" for being in the video, as "they didn't have the full support of their families" because they were in a same-sex relationship.)

Both engagements are artistic: Matt handcrafts elaborate dioramas from Post-it Notes that illustrate his relationship with Chelsea, while Aly meticulously paints posters that illustrate her love story with Andrea. The video follows each couple as the engagements happen; at both, Bareilles naturally shows up and plays "I Choose You." Unsurprisingly, it's impossible to watch the clip without tearing up because every moment is so special.

Top 10 Misunderstood Love Songs

Once you start digging into lyrics and song origin stories, as it turns out, not all love songs are . . . actually love songs at all.

1. Sara Bareilles, "Love Song"

The pianist was frustrated by demands from her record label—so she wrote a song all about how she wasn't going to deliver the romantic goods, in a songwriting sense.

2. The Beatles, "Martha My Dear"

There are a surprising number of love songs about pets. In fact, Paul McCartney wrote this sweet, affectionate song about his sheepdog named Martha.

3. Blondie, "One Way or Another"

Although this jaunty song seems like a lighthearted tune about romantic pursuit, Debbie Harry actually wrote this Blondie classic after a rather scary real-life situation: a stalker.

4. Mariah Carey, "Always Be My Baby"

This bittersweet tune isn't an expression of fidelity but a tune about goodbyes; more specifically, the narrator is saying a fond farewell to an ex—at least for now.

5. Phil Collins, "In the Air Tonight"

The onetime Genesis drummer wrote this song interrogating his feelings after getting a divorce—it's much more about turbulent love than reciprocating love.

6. Daryl Hall and John Oates, "Kiss on My List"

Bad news for anyone who has this tune on their love song playlist: Hall has said that this song isn't about a romance—but more about deflating someone's ego, because a kiss is just *one thing* on someone's list.

7. The Police, "Every Breath You Take"

This isn't a song about the lovely experience of watching a beloved breathe—it's a tune squarely about obsession.

8. R.E.M., "The One I Love"

Vocalist Michael Stipe dedicated this tune to someone he loves, but there's a catch: The tone is sarcastic, as he later clarifies this person is merely a placeholder taking up space. Ouch!

9. U2, "One"

The members of U2 have long said that this meditative *Achtung Baby* ballad isn't about unity and togetherness—but realizing that we have to coexist despite differences.

10. Dionne Warwick, "I Say a Little Prayer"

Popularized by soul great Dionne Warwick, this iconic Hal David–Burt Bacharach composition is really about having compassion for (and sending good thoughts to) young soldiers shipping off to serve in the Vietnam War.

ALL OF ME

2013 • JOHN LEGEND

Songwriters: Toby Gad and John Legend

LOOK IN THE dictionary under the term "fairy-tale romance" and you'll find photos of musician John Legend and supermodel-turned-entrepreneur Chrissy Teigen. The couple first met in 2007 when Legend was shooting a video for his song "Stereo" and Teigen was cast as the love interest.

"I walked into John's dressing room to meet him, and he was ironing in his underwear," Teigen told *Cosmopolitan* in 2014. "I said, 'You do your own ironing!?' He said, 'Of course I do.' I gave him a hug." After the shoot, the duo ate In-N-Out burgers and hooked up—setting the stage for their eventual happily ever after. Married since 2013, the A-list couple now has four adorable children and frequently documents their beautiful lives together on social media.

Unsurprisingly, Legend wrote the delicate piano ballad "All of Me" for Teigen, at collaborator Toby Gad's Los Angeles studio. "The first time I sang it for Chrissy, I whispered it in her ear and she cried," Legend wrote in a 2023 Instagram reminiscence. It's easy to hear why: The song's lyrics are vulnerable and deeply romantic but describe a realistic approach to love. He praises Teigen's flaws and strengths, expresses love for her fiery personality, and says he'll support her in good *and* tough times. She's not some untouchable perfect goddess—but a real person he loves inside *and* out.

"All of Me" reached No. 1 on the *Billboard* Hot 100 in May 2014 and has since become a favorite song for wedding first dances. Fittingly, Teigen was also featured in the song's music video, reprising the appearance that brought her and Legend together in the first place. The clip ended with real-life footage of the couple's wedding in Lake Como, Italy—where he sang "All of Me" at the reception.

The song has grown into something that's much more than Legend's wedding gift to Teigen. A remix of the song featuring the superstar DJ/producer Tiësto won a Grammy Award for Best Remixed Recording, Non-Classical, while Jennifer Nettles and special guest Hunter Hayes issued a country version. "I'm so grateful for what this song has meant to my life," Legend wrote on Instagram, "but also for what it's meant to you."

CHEEK TO CHEEK

2014 • TONY BENNETT AND LADY GAGA

Songwriter: Irving Berlin

EVERYONE KNOWS PHYSICAL activities like dancing are good for your heart health—in more ways than one. That's the theory posited by the standard "Cheek to Cheek," which serves as a love letter to romance *and* slow dancing. High-impact activities like fishing in a river or mountain climbing can't compare to the adrenaline rush of being close on a dance floor. In fact, the "Cheek to Cheek" narrator says they're blissfully happy—akin to being in heaven—while dancing.

Penned by the legendary Irving Berlin—the composer also responsible for standards such as "White Christmas," "Puttin' on the Ritz" and "There's No Business Like Show Business"—"Cheek to Cheek" made its debut in the 1935 movie *Top Hat* starring Fred Astaire and Ginger Rogers. Berlin wrote six new songs for the film and was said to have penned "Cheek to Cheek" in just one night.

In the movie, Astaire croons the song to Rogers in a languid and delighted tone, relishing in the intimacy and romance of a slow dance. Astaire's recording of the song with the Leo Reisman Orchestra was a huge success. The song spent five weeks at No. 1 on Your Hit Parade, a popular radio countdown show of the time, and was nominated for an Oscar for Best Song. Sixty-five years after its release, Astaire's 1935 version was inducted into the Grammy Hall of Fame.

Hundreds of artists have covered "Cheek to Cheek" over the years, including Frank Sinatra, Doris Day, Ella Fitzgerald, and Taco. The song was also the title track on the 2014 album by Tony Bennett and Lady Gaga. Although an unlikely duo on paper—he was a legendary silver-fox crooner, she was a colorful modern pop star—they found common ground covering jazz standards.

In the hands of Gaga and Bennett, "Cheek to Cheek" was snappy and upbeat—a far cry from the rendition that appeared in *Top Hat*. The vocalists banter back and forth with gleeful bravado atop classic jazz accompaniment performed by a red-hot troupe that's clearly at the top of their game.

The song helped propel the success of the album *Cheek to Cheek*; among other things, it won a Grammy Award for Best Traditional Pop Vocal Album. Gaga and Bennett also cemented a creative partnership that transcended generations—and embraced love. In a beautiful Instagram post after Bennett's 2023 death, Gaga remembered her duet partner. "With Tony, I got to live my life in a time warp," she wrote. "Tony and I had this magical power. We transported ourselves to another era, modernized the music together, and gave it all new life as a singing duo."

PERFECT DUET

2017 · ED SHEERAN FEATURING BEYONCÉ

Songwriter: Ed Sheeran

ED SHEERAN IS uncommonly good at writing love songs. There's "Shape of You," about turning a lust-driven meet-cute at a bar into a real relationship, and "Everything Has Changed," a duet with Taylor Swift that speaks to the moment your life gets turned upside down by someone else. And then there's the love-me-until-we're-old-and-gray ballad "Thinking Out Loud," which is widely considered one of the best wedding first dance songs of all time.

When it came time to write 2017's swaying waltz "Perfect," Sheeran said he wanted to best one song—"Thinking Out Loud." In an interview with the radio DJ Zane Lowe, Sheeran clarified what he meant: "With 'Perfect,' it was like, 'I need to write the best love song of my career.'"

"Perfect" indeed features a love story that unfolds over time and focuses on what matters: small moments of tenderness between two people, like sharing a romantic dance together in the dark. The couple are on the same page about what they want out of life—sharing dreams, having kids, making a home together—which builds trust and tenderness. Sheeran also inserts important details—like the fact that the couple are barefoot while dancing—that bring the song to life.

Inspiration struck Sheeran at singer James Blunt's house. One line from "Perfect," about a couple having a romantic moment while sharing a beloved tune, grew out of Sheeran and Blunt listening to "March Madness" by the rapper Future. Another line, about finding your person when you were a kid, also spurred his creativity. "I had that and I was like, right, let me just flesh that out," he told Lowe. "And the song happened and was sort of finished that day. I knew it was special."

Fittingly, Sheeran stuck to elegant instrumentation highlighted by low-key guitar and an arrangement of strings and woodwinds that bloom into a gorgeous backdrop. In the UK, "Perfect" ended up reaching No. 4 in early 2017. But Sheeran wasn't done trying to make the song, well, perfect: In December 2017, he issued a stripped-back acoustic remix, "Perfect Duet," featuring Beyoncé. She took lead on one of the verses, subtly flipping several of the lyrics so they came from her perspective. This version was even more successful, becoming the UK's prestigious Christmas No. 1 in 2017 and also topping the US *Billboard* Hot 100.

ADORE YOU

2019 • HARRY STYLES

Songwriters: Amy Allen, Tyler Johnson, Kid Harpoon, Harry Styles

ONE DIRECTION'S CATALOG overflows with songs about loving someone for who they are—not who you *want* them to be. Perhaps the group's most famous love songs are "What Makes You Beautiful," a fizzy tune about letting a shy person know they're gorgeous, and the Ed Sheeran–written "Little Things"; the latter finds the group showering a beloved one with compliments.

When 1D member Harry Styles went solo, he continued with the summery seduction on breezy tracks like 2019's "Watermelon Sugar," which extols the virtues of a steamy, sweet love affair. ("It's also about the female orgasm but totally different," Styles said during a 2021 concert. "It's not really relevant.")

That same year, Styles released "Adore You," which has a similar message: The narrator is only interested in worshiping—and, one presumes, giving pleasure to—someone they think is beautiful. The song's lyrics are respectful, of course; it's implied that "Adore You" is a song about asking permission to dole out love and affection.

Conceptually, "Adore You" is "kind of similar to what 'Watermelon Sugar' is about—that initial excitement of meeting someone," Styles said during his NPR Tiny Desk concert. Fittingly for a song based on the intoxicating experience of having a crush, Styles wrote "Adore You" and several other songs "in a burst of inspiration" as the recording sessions were winding down.

Production and co-writing came from Tyler Johnson and Kid Harpoon, while Amy Allen, who co-wrote hits for Halsey ("Without Me") and Selena Gomez ("Back to You"), also did the co-writing honors here. Together with Styles, the team crafted a song that feels like the aural equivalent to sitting on a beach watching the sunset.

Funky rhythms, falsetto vocal harmonies, and prickly electric guitar exude a vibe that's somewhere between manicured '70s rock and warm '80s pop—all carried by Styles's exuberant, sparkling vocals.

"'Adore You' is the poppiest song on the album," he told *Rolling Stone* in 2019. "This time I really felt so much less afraid to write fun pop songs." After name-checking several favorite songwriters known for their serious work (including Harry Nilsson, Paul Simon, and Van Morrison), Styles praised the idea of thematic balance, adding, "And I think, well, Van Morrison has 'Brown Eyed Girl' and Nilsson has 'Coconut.' Bowie has 'Let's Dance.' The fun stuff is important."

"Adore You" reached the top 10 in the US and UK, won a 2021 ASCAP Pop Music Award, and became one of BMI's Most Performed Songs of the Year. The song's music video, meanwhile, was nominated for a Grammy Award.

Acknowledgments

It was such a joy to delve into the world of love songs and write this book! Thanks to my editor Jordana Hawkins, art director Katie Benezra, illustrator Darling Clementine, publisher Kristin Kiser, publicist Seta Zink, marketer Elizabeth Parks, production editor Melanie Gold, managing editor Jess Riordan, and everyone at Running Press for their care, diligence, and support in shepherding this book to publication.

Sources

All artist names and song titles were found via the original artwork published at Discogs (discogs.com) or on the streaming platform Apple Music. Chart positions were verified via *Billboard* issues published at World Radio History (worldradiohistory.com), and UK charts were found at Official Album Charts (officialcharts.com). Other information was verified at the Internet Movie Database (imdb.com), the Guinness World Records website (guinnessworldrecords.com), the lyrics site genius.com, and via YouTube (youtube.com).

LISTS

Huhn, Mary. "Blue-Eyed Soul—White Soul Duo Hall & Oates Get Their Due." *New York Post*, March 14, 2004.

Uitti, Jacob. "Behind the Song Lyrics: Dionne Warwick's 'I Say a Little Prayer' by Burt Bacharach and Hal David." *American Songwriter*, 2021.

FRED ASTAIRE, "THE WAY YOU LOOK TONIGHT" (1936)

Skolsky, Sidney. "Hollywood." *Tampa Tribune*, October 11, 1936.

Wilk, Max. *They're Playing Our Song: Conversations with America's Classic Songwriters*. New York: Da Capo Press, 1997.

NAT KING COLE, "UNFORGETTABLE" (1951)

Buskin, Richard. "Classic Tracks: Natalie Cole & Nat 'King' Cole 'Unforgettable.'" *Sound on Sound*, January 2004.

ELLA FITZGERALD, "LET'S DO IT (LET'S FALL IN LOVE)" (1956)

Bundy, June. "Mr. J. Q. Grows Up; He's Less Prudish About Music on Air." *Billboard*, December 25, 1954.

Porter, Cole. *The Complete Lyrics of Cole Porter*. Edited by Robert Kimball. New York: Da Capo Press, 1992.

Tyler, Don. *Hit Songs, 1900–1955: American Popular Music of the Pre-Rock Era*. Jefferson, NC: McFarland, 2007.

THE FIVE SATINS, "IN THE STILL OF THE NIGHT" (1956)

"A Love Letter Set to Music." *Smithsonian Magazine*, as published in the *Daily Advertiser* (Lafayette, LA), June 7, 2004.

"Reviews of New R&B Records." *Billboard*, June 9, 1956.

Zaretsky, Mark. "Fred Parris & His Satins Return to St. Bernadette's in New Haven for PBS Filming." *New Haven Register*, December 1, 2017.

PEGGY LEE, "FEVER" (1958)

Kettner, Klaus with Tony Wilkinson. "Eddie Cooley." BlackCat Rockabilly. https://web.archive.org/web/20061011074316/https://www.rockabilly.nl/references/messages/eddie_cooley.htm.

Martindale, Wink. "Peggy Lee Audio Book." https://www.youtube.com/watch?v=oAzLT2A1oyk.

Santiago, Iván. "The Peggy Lee Bio-Discography: Observations About the Song 'Fever.'" November 11, 2021. https://peggyleediscography.com/p/LeeResearchFever.php.

Simon, Scott. "Delving into Peggy Lee's Steamy Mystique." NPR Music, May 6, 2006.

"WILD Jock Runs 'Fever' 42½ Hours." *Billboard*, August 25, 1958.

PAUL ANKA, "PUT YOUR HEAD ON MY SHOULDER" (1959)

Anka, Paul. *My Way.* New York: St. Martin's Press, 2013.

Rotella, Mark. "Put Your Head on His Shoulder: PW Talks with Paul Anka." *Publishers Weekly*, March 29, 2013.

THE FLAMINGOS, "I ONLY HAVE EYES FOR YOU" (1959)

Professor of Rock. "The Flamingos' Surviving Member on Creating OLDIES Hit I Only Have Eyes for You." https://www.youtube.com/watch?v=6_GidEL_blU.

"The 500 Greatest Songs of All Time." *Rolling Stone*, September 15, 2021.

BILLIE HOLIDAY, "LOVE IS HERE TO STAY" (1959)

Gower, Melrose. "Swing's High." *Cincinnati Enquirer*, February 28, 1937.

Wilcox, Grace. "The Hollywood Reporter." *Nashville Banner*, September 5, 1937.

SAM COOKE, "WONDERFUL WORLD" (1960)

Guralnick, Peter. *Dream Boogie: The Triumph of Sam Cooke.* New York: Back Bay Books, 2006.

ETTA JAMES, "AT LAST" (1960)

"Salvage 'At Last' Tune from Cutting Room Floor; In New Miller Picture." *Variety*, July 1942.

PATSY CLINE, "I FALL TO PIECES" (1961)

Nassour, Ellis. *Honky Tonk Angel: The Intimate Story of Patsy Cline.* New York: St. Martin's Press, 1993.

"Patsy Cline, 'I Fall to Pieces.'" HarlanHoward.com.

ELVIS PRESLEY, "CAN'T HELP FALLING IN LOVE" (1961)

"March 23, 1961" session. Keith Flynn's Elvis Presley Pages. https://keithflynn.com/recording-sessions/610323.html#001.

RAY CHARLES, "I CAN'T STOP LOVING YOU" (1962)

"Country Legend Don Gibson Dies." Associated Press, November 5, 2003.

Horstman, Dorothy. *Sing Your Heart Out, Country Boy.* New York: Dutton, 1975.

MARTHA AND THE VANDELLAS, "HEAT WAVE" (1963)

Martha Reeves & the Vandellas inductee page. The Motown Museum. https://www.motownmuseum.org/artist/martha-and-the-vandellas/.

Dozier, Lamont. About "(Love Is Like a) Heat Wave." https://web.archive.org/web/20040606030823/https://lamontdozier.com/lyrics.html.

THE RONETTES, "BE MY BABY" (1963)

Brown, Mick. *Tearing Down the Wall of Sound: The Rise and Fall of Phil Spector.* London: Bloomsbury, 2007.

Buskin, Richard. "Classic Tracks: The Ronettes, 'Be My Baby.'" *Sound on Sound*, April 2007.

Simpson, Dave. "How We Made the Ronettes' 'Be My Baby.'" *Guardian*, November 17, 2015.

FRANK SINATRA, "FLY ME TO THE MOON" (1964)

Apollo Flight Journal. "Apollo 10: day 2, part 8: Mid-course correction and TV transmission." history.nasa.gov/afj/ap10fj/as10-day2-pt8.html.

Chilton, Martin. "Moon Landing Mystery: Did Buzz Aldrin Really Play Frank Sinatra on the Moon?" *Independent* (UK), July 18, 2019.

Holden, Stephen. "Bart Howard, 88, Songwriter Known for 'Fly Me to the Moon.'" *New York Times*, February 23, 2004.

Longden, Tom. "Bart Howard." *Des Moines Register*. https://archive.ph/20131207062000/http://data.desmoinesregister.com/dmr/famous-iowans/bart-howard.

Martin, Michel. "50 Years Later, Looking Back at Apollo 10, Precursor to the Moon Landing." *All Things Considered*, NPR. May 18, 2019.

McGlynn, Lawrence. "Music to the Moon: The Apollo X Music Tape." *Space Artifacts* blog, December 2014. https://www.spaceartifactsarchive.com/2014/12/music-to-the-moon-the-apollo-x-music-tape.html.

THE TEMPTATIONS, "MY GIRL" (1964)

Blair, Elizabeth. "'My Girl.'" *Weekend Edition Sunday*, NPR, June 4, 2000.

"The Temptations, 'My Girl.'" SongFacts.

MARY WELLS, "MY GUY" (1964)

Benjaminson, Peter. *Mary Wells: The Tumultuous Life of Motown's First Superstar*. Chicago: Chicago Review Press, 2012.

Caulfield, Keith. "50 Years Ago: Motown Records' First No. 1 Single." *Billboard*, May 16, 2014.

THE RIGHTEOUS BROTHERS, "UNCHAINED MELODY" (1965)

Garber, Megan. "How 'Unchained Melody' Broke Free." *Atlantic*, July 13, 2015.

Martin, Douglas. "Hy Zaret, 99, Tin Pan Alley Lyricist, Is Dead." *New York Times*, July 3, 2007.

Medley, Bill. *The Time of My Life: A Righteous Brother's Memoir*. New York: Da Capo Press, 2014.

"Theatre Tunes Comprise a Fourth of ASCAP's Top Songs/Musical Works in 20th Century." *Playbill*, August 28, 1999.

SONNY AND CHER, "I GOT YOU BABE" (1965)

Altham, Keith. "Sonny and Cher: We're in Love, That's The Secret of Success." *New Musical Express Annual*, 1966.

Caulfield, Keith. "Cher Reflects on 50 Years on the Billboard Charts: 'I Got You Babe,' 'Believe' & Beyond." *Billboard*, August 7, 2015.

Cher with Coplon, Jeff. *The First Time*. New York: Simon & Schuster, 1998.

"I Got You Babe" recording contract. https://web.archive.org/web/20220220212922/https://www.wreckingcrewfilm.com/afmcontracts/Sonny+Cher_IGotYouBabe.pdf.

BEACH BOYS, "GOD ONLY KNOWS" (1966)

Deevoy, Adrian. "Beach Boy Brian Wilson: 'Punk Rock? I Don't Know What That Is.'" *Guardian*, April 9, 2015.

"Sir Paul McCartney Cries When He Hears 'God Only Knows.'" LondonNet, September 19, 2007.

Wenzel, John. "Brian Wilson on Weed Legalization, What He Thinks of His 'Love & Mercy' Biopic." *Denver Post*, July 2, 2015, https://www.denverpost.com/2015/07/02/brian-wilson-on-weed-legalization-what-he-thinks-of-his-love-mercy-biopic/.

THE MONKEES, "I'M A BELIEVER" (1966)

The Monkees. "Dance, Monkee, Dance," season 1, episode 14, December 12, 1966. https://youtu.be/IHB6L0ZPxXI.

The Monkees. *More of the Monkees*, Rhino Records, deluxe edition, 2006.

Simmons, Sylvie. Interview with Neil Diamond. *Mojo*, July 2008.

"Single Stories: The Monkees, 'I'm a Believer.'" Rhino.com, October 15, 2018.

OTIS REDDING, "TRY A LITTLE TENDERNESS" (1966)

Bowman, Robert M. J. *Soulsville, U.S.A.: The Story of Stax Records.* New York: Schirmer Books, 1997.

"Otis Redding's Final Performance." *Upbeat*, December 9, 1967. https://www.youtube.com/watch?v=RYOtDq3NUJA.

Robinson, Elsie. "Listen, World." *Charlotte Observer*, April 18, 1933.

PERCY SLEDGE, "WHEN A MAN LOVES A WOMAN" (1966)

Abbey, John. "Percy Sledge." *Blues & Soul*, 1970.

Eldridge, Royston. "Percy Sledge: Have Percy!" *Melody Maker*, 1969.

Hackett, Vernell. "Writers Pen Only One Hit: But . . . 'When a Man Loves a Woman' Is a Definite Hit." *American Songwriter*, 1994.

"Percy Sledge Biography." Rock & Roll Hall of Fame, April 2015. Rockhall.com.

Wake, Matt. "'When a Man Loves a Woman': 50th Anniversary of Recording that Defined Muscle Shoals Sound." Alabama Media Group, February 17, 2016.

ARETHA FRANKLIN, "(YOU MAKE ME FEEL LIKE) A NATURAL WOMAN" (1967)

King, Carole. *A Natural Woman.* New York: Grand Central, 2012.

Remnick, David. "Soul Survivor: The Revival and Hidden Treasure of Aretha Franklin." *New Yorker*, March 28, 2016.

MARVIN GAYE AND TAMMI TERRELL, "AIN'T NO MOUNTAIN HIGH ENOUGH" (1967)

Kot, Greg. "Valerie Simpson on Nick Ashford: 'I'm Not Used to Him Not Being Here Yet.'" *Chicago Tribune*, November 17, 2011.

FRANKIE VALLI, "CAN'T TAKE MY EYES OFF YOU" (1967)

Barnes, Terry. "Sony in the House." *Billboard*, March 27, 1999.

MacIntosh, Dan. Interview with Bob Gaudio. SongFacts, January 20, 2015.

Monaghan, John. "Roostertail Has a Role in 'Jersey Boys.'" *Detroit Free Press*, December 17, 2009.

Willman, Chris. "Frankie Valli on Jersey Boys and His Unlikely Success: 'The Way I Grew Up, It Was Basically Against All Odds.'" *Parade*, June 6, 2014.

THE BEATLES, "SOMETHING" (1969)

Boyd, Pattie with Penny Junor. *Wonderful Today: The Autobiography.* London: Headline Review, 2007.

Interview with George Harrison, October 8, 1969. beatlesinterviews.org/db1969.1008.beatles.html.

Kendall, Jo. "Pattie Boyd: My Life in 10 Songs." *Classic Rock*, December 8, 2022.

Stevens, Jenny. "'I Was a Bad Influence on the Beatles': James Taylor on Lennon, Love and Recovery." *Guardian*, February 17, 2020.

Yorke, Ritchie. "George Harrison Talks About the Beatles' Album 'Abbey Road.'" *Detroit Free Press*, September 26, 1969.

ROBERTA FLACK, "THE FIRST TIME EVER I SAW YOUR FACE" (1969)

De Yampert, Rick. Kristin M. Hall, "Grammy Winning Artists Reflect on What Makes a Song a Hit," AP News, January 23, 2018, https://apnews.com/music-aa6118fdbf324b23aec794c066a75e15.

Peggy Seeger Facebook post. March 20, 2023.

Peggy Seeger Facebook video. "Scenes from a Life—The First Time Ever I Saw Your Face." March 26, 2023.

"Roberta Flack, 'The First Time Ever I Saw Your Face.'" SuperSeventies.com/1972_8singles.html.

THE JACKSON 5, "I'LL BE THERE" (1970)
"75 Greatest Boy Band Songs of All Time."
Rolling Stone, July 27, 2020.

PAUL MCCARTNEY, "MAYBE I'M AMAZED" (1970)
Billboard staff. "Paul McCartney on His
Not-So-Silly Love Songs," *Billboard*,
March 16, 2001.
"Maybe I'm Amazed." The Paul McCartney
Project. https://www.the-paulmccartney-
project.com/song/maybe-im-amazed/.

STEVIE WONDER, "SIGNED, SEALED, DELIVERED (I'M YOURS)" (1970)
Interview with Syreeta Wright, 1974.
https://www.youtube.com/
watch?v=wufKm3OdTow.
Perone, James E. *The Sound of Stevie
Wonder: His Words and Music.*
Westport, CT: Praeger, 2006.
Sexton, Paul. "'Signed, Sealed, Delivered
I'm Yours': Stevie Wonder's Dynamite
Dispatch." UDiscover Music, June 30,
2023.

JONI MITCHELL, "A CASE OF YOU" (1971)
Crowe, Cameron. "Joni Mitchell Defends
Herself." *Rolling Stone*, July 26, 1979.
Hilburn, Robert. "An Art Born of Pain,
an Artist in Happy Exile." *Los Angeles
Times*, September 5, 2004.

AL GREEN, "LET'S STAY TOGETHER" (1972)
Eldredge, Richard. "Al Green's Sweet Soul
Reunion." *Palm Beach Post*, December
14, 2003.

JOE COCKER, "YOU ARE SO BEAUTIFUL" (1974)
Stebbins, Jon. *Dennis Wilson: The Real
Beach Boy.* Toronto: ECW Press, 2000.
Sutcliffe, Phil. "Joe Cocker." *Mojo*, 2010.

CAPTAIN & TENNILLE, "LOVE WILL KEEP US TOGETHER" (1975)
"Neil Sedaka, 'Love Will Keep Us
Together.'" SongFacts.

Shaffer, Paul. "Neil Sedaka Talks with
Paul Shaffer About 'Love Will Keep
Us Together' and Captain & Tennille."
SiriusXM, April 2020. https://www.
youtube.com/watch?v=fTw9yGphAxg.

ELVIN BISHOP, "FOOLED AROUND AND FELL IN LOVE" (1975)
Bishop, Elvin. "Fooled Around and Fell in
Love." AllMusic.
Wiser, Carl. Interview with Elvin Bishop.
SongFacts, September 13, 2007.

MINNIE RIPERTON, "LOVIN' YOU" (1975)
Eskow, Gary. "Classic Tracks: Minnie
Riperton's 'Lovin' You.'" *Mix*, February
1, 2008.

BEE GEES, "HOW DEEP IS YOUR LOVE" (1977)
Bilyeu, Melinda, Hector Cook, and Andrew
Môn Hughes. *The Bee Gees: Tales of The
Brothers Gibb.* London: Omnibus Press,
2011.
White, Timothy. "This Is Where We Came In."
Billboard tribute edition, "The Bee Gees:
35 Years of Music," March 24, 2001.

BILLY JOEL, "JUST THE WAY YOU ARE" (1977)
DeVault, Russ. "Joel Phasing Out Arena
Shows for Smaller, Intimate Settings."
Atlanta Journal-Constitution, January
28, 1994.
Howard Stern Show, November 16, 2010.
https://www.youtube.com/watch?v=n1-
kLcvMLiY.
Interview with Phil Ramone. https://www.
youtube.com/watch?v=rSxY_a7McXw.
O'Hare, Kevin. "Billy Joel—The Republican
Interview." MassLive, July 6, 2008.

RUPERT HOLMES, "ESCAPE (THE PIÑA COLADA SONG)" (1979)
James, Gary. Interview with Rupert
Holmes. http://www.classicbands.com/
RupertHolmesInterview.html.
Yarnell, Laurie. "The Man Who Wrote 'The
Piña Colada Song' Lives Locally in Cold
Spring." *Hudson Valley*, July 12, 2019.

DARYL HALL AND JOHN OATES, "YOU MAKE MY DREAMS" (1980)

MacIntosh, Dan. Interview with John Oates. SongFacts, April 7, 2011.

Savage, Mark. "Hall and Oates: How You Make My Dreams Became a Streaming Colossus." BBC, June 8, 2021.

Wiser, Carl. "Daryl Hall: 'There's Another Way of Looking at the World.'" SongFacts, February 19, 2015.

"You Make My Dreams (Come True) Hits 1 Billion Streams." JohnOates.com, October 14, 2020.

QUEEN, "CRAZY LITTLE THING CALLED LOVE" (1979)

Coleman, Ray. "The Man Who Would Be Queen." *Melody Maker*, May 2, 1981.

Interview with Brian May. Absolute Radio, August 17, 2011. https://www.youtube.com/watch?v=rvGlDkQqxoc.

Interview with Roger Taylor. "Cologne Audio Press Kit," 2004. https://archive.ph/20120721083734/http://www.brianmay.com/queen/queennews/queennewsnov04.html#selection-2357.556-2357.596.

GROVER WASHINGTON JR. FEATURING BILL WITHERS, "JUST THE TWO OF US" (1980)

Interview with Bill Withers. *Merv Griffin Show*, 1981. https://www.youtube.com/watch?v=FkietDNYBFs.

Meschino, Patricia. "Ralph MacDonald, Master Percussionist, Grammy-Award Winning Songwriter, Dead At 67." *Billboard*, December 27, 2011.

Wiser, Carl. Interview with Bill Withers. SongFacts, January 2, 2004.

JOURNEY, "DON'T STOP BELIEVIN'" (1981)

Condran, Ed. "Journey's Jonathan Cain Shares the Real-Life Story Behind 'Don't Stop Believin'' as Band Prepares for Spokane Show." *Spokesman-Review* (Spokane, WA), April 13, 2023.

"Steve Perry Reveals How He Wrote "Don't Stop Believin'." Jonesy's Jukebox, October 2, 2018. https://www.youtube.com/watch?v=CnXwFUuoylw.

Tucker, Neely, "That Night in Detroit: Journey's 'Don't Stop Believin'.'" *Timeless Stories from the Library of Congress* blog, April 13, 2022.

LIONEL RICHIE AND DIANA ROSS, "ENDLESS LOVE" (1981)

Bream, Jon. "Songwriter Finds Theme of Success in 'Endless Love.'" *Minneapolis Star*, February 24, 1982.

MARVIN GAYE, "SEXUAL HEALING" (1982)

Kawashima, Dale. "Amazing Saga: The Story of How Author David Ritz Wrote the Classic Hit Song 'Sexual Healing' with Marvin Gaye." SongwriterUniverse. https://www.songwriteruniverse.com/davidritz.htm.

Norris, Chris. "The 808 Heard Round the World." *New Yorker*, August 13, 2015.

Smith, Mat. "Marvin Gaye 'Sexual Healing.'" *Electronic Sound*. https://www.electronicsound.co.uk/time-machine/marvin-gaye-sexual-healing/.

Williams, Chris. "'The Man Was a Genius': Tales from Making Marvin Gaye's Final Album." *Atlantic*, October 1, 2012.

WILLIE NELSON, "ALWAYS ON MY MIND" (1982)

Hilburn, Robert. "The Surprising Saga of 'Always on My Mind.'" *Los Angeles Times*, April 24, 1988.

Nelson, Willie, and Bud Shrake. *Willie: An Autobiography*. New York: Cooper Square Press, 2000.

CYNDI LAUPER, "TIME AFTER TIME" (1983)

Myers, Marc. "How Cyndi Lauper Wrote Her First No. 1 Hit, 'Time After Time.'" *Wall Street Journal*, December 1, 2015.

DOLLY PARTON AND KENNY ROGERS, "ISLANDS IN THE STREAM" (1983)

"Kenny Rogers and Dolly Parton, 'Islands in the Stream.'" SongFacts.

Newman, Melinda. "Barry Gibb on Reuniting with Dolly Parton & Who He 'Freaked Out' Over While Recording New Country Duets Album." *Billboard*, January 5, 2021.

FOREIGNER, "I WANT TO KNOW WHAT LOVE IS" (1984)

Giles, Jeff. "Foreigner's Mick Jones Looks Back on 'I Want to Know What Love Is.'" Ultimate Classic Rock, December 27, 2013. https://ultimateclassicrock.com/foreigner-i-want-to-know-what-love-is/.

Jones, Mick. "I Wrote That: Foreigner—I Want to Know What Love Is." *M* magazine, October 7, 2014.

Quinlan, Michael. "Foreigner Switched to a Ballad for Latest Single—but Fear Not, They'll Rock at the Derby Eve Jam." *Courier-Journal* (Louisville, KY), May 3, 1985.

Wiser, Carl. Interview with Mick Jones. SongFacts, October 23, 2009.

HUEY LEWIS AND THE NEWS, "THE POWER OF LOVE" (1985)

Bronson, Fred. *The Billboard Book of Number One Hits*. New York: Billboard Publications, 1988.

Zaleski, Annie. "'The Power of Love' Gave Huey Lewis and the News Pop Culture Immortality." A.V. Club, May 26, 2015.

MADONNA, "CRAZY FOR YOU" (1985)

Bronson, Fred. *The Billboard Book of Number One Hits*. New York: Billboard Publications, 2003.

"Rob Mounsey interview, Part 2." *80sography* podcast, December 22, 2022.

SIMPLE MINDS, "DON'T YOU (FORGET ABOUT ME)" (1985)

Rutherford, Kevin. "Simple Minds' '80s Classic 'Don't You (Forget About Me)' Returns to Charts Thanks to Super Bowl Ad." *Billboard*, February 25, 2022.

Simpson, Dave. "Bryan Ferry: 'I Did a Lot of Whistling on my Paper Round as a Lad.'" *Guardian*, April 28, 2022.

Simpson, Dave. "Simple Minds: How We Made Don't You (Forget About Me)." *Guardian*, November 15, 2016.

Sturges, Fiona. "Don't You (Forget About Me)—Simple Minds Have Had a Fraught Relationship with Their Biggest Hit." *Financial Times*, September 2, 2019.

Zaleski, Annie. "Danke schön! 'The John Hughes Mixtapes' Sheds Light on Vibrant and Essential Movie Soundtrack Gems." *Salon*, November 26, 2022.

BERLIN, "TAKE MY BREATH AWAY" (1986)

Simpson, Dave. "How We Made: Take My Breath Away, the Top Gun Theme Tune by Berlin." *Guardian*, November 16, 2020.

"Remember *Top Gun*'s song 'Take My Breath Away' in 1986? Exclusive Interview with John Crawford." Shortlisted. the-shortlisted.co.uk/take-my-breath-away-top-gun-berlin-interview.

"Take My Breath Away (demo)." https://web.archive.org/web/20160125225439/http://themotels.com/2013/06/05/take-my-breath-away-demo/.

PETER GABRIEL, "IN YOUR EYES" (1986)

Greene, Andy. "Q&A: Peter Gabriel Reflects on His 1986 Landmark Album 'So.'" *Rolling Stone*, September 4, 2012.

"Peter Gabriel—New Blood—In Your Eyes." 2011. https://www.youtube.com/watch?v=aNrpCQG3HBE.

PRINCE AND THE REVOLUTION, "KISS" (1986)

Daley, Dan. "Classic Tracks: Prince, 'Kiss.'" *Mix*, June 1, 2001.

"Kiss." Prince Vault. https://princevault.com/index.php?title=Kiss.

"Prince, 'Kiss,'" demo. https://www.youtube.com/watch?v=oSm9voCZ_L4.

Williams, Chris. "The Mountain." Wax Poetics, April 20, 2021. https://www.waxpoetics.com/connections/prince/article/prince-susan-rogers-david-z-the-mountain/.

FLEETWOOD MAC, "EVERYWHERE" (1987)

Male, Andrew. "Christine McVie Remembered: 'I'm Good at Pathos. I Write About Romantic Despair a Lot.'" *Mojo*, 2017.

GUNS N' ROSES, "SWEET CHILD O' MINE" (1987)

Elliott, Paul. "What the Unstoppable Rise of Guns N' Roses Looked Like from the Inside..." *Classic Rock*, May 8, 2017.

Hiatt, Brian. "Guns N' Roses' 'Appetite for Destruction': Filthy, Sexy, Cool." *Rolling Stone*, August 9, 2007.

"The Story Behind the Song—Guns N' Roses, 'Sweet Child O' Mine.'" *Q*, December 2005.

U2, "WITH OR WITHOUT YOU" (1987)

Breskin, David. "Bono: The Rolling Stone Interview." *Rolling Stone*, October 8, 1987.

McCormick, Neil. *U2 by U2*. New York: Harper Collins, 2006.

INXS, "NEVER TEAR US APART," (1988)

"Milestones: Remembering INXS's Michael Hutchence on His 50th Birthday." Slicing Up Eyeballs, January 22, 2010.

"The 500 Greatest Songs of All Time." *Rolling Stone*, September 15, 2021.

"Thousands Attend Service for INXS Singer." *Tampa Bay Times*, November 28, 1997.

Pidgeon, John. "INXS: *Kick*." Book Excerpt, 1991. http://www.rocksbackpages.com.eresources.cuyahogalibrary.org/Library/Article/inxs-ikicki.

RICHARD MARX, "RIGHT HERE WAITING" (1989)

"I Definitely Know About Shilpa Shetty: Richard Marx." *Indian Express*, February 20, 2010.

"Richard Marx Grateful Barbra Streisand Rejected His Song." Cover Media, July 7, 2021.

TINA TURNER, "THE BEST" (1989)

Sutherland, Mark. "I've Made Lots of Money Doing Something I Love, but There's Such a Lack of Respect." Music Business Worldwide, January 3, 2023.

Wiser, Carl. Interview with Holly Knight. SongFacts, June 17, 2021.

THE CURE, "FRIDAY I'M IN LOVE" (1992)

Interview with the Cure, Discogs.

"The Cure's Robert Smith Interview— Part Two." *NME*, October 29, 2008. https://www.femalefirst.co.uk/music/interviews/Robert+Smith-59117.html.

WHITNEY HOUSTON, "I WILL ALWAYS LOVE YOU" (1992)

Interview with Patti LaBelle. iloveoldschoolmusic.com.

Paulson, Dave. "Dolly Parton Remembers Writing 'I Will Always Love You.'" *Tennessean*, December 26, 2015.

DURAN DURAN, "COME UNDONE" (1993)

"After Nearly Drowning Last Summer, Duran Duran's Simon Le Bon Tests Matrimonial Waters." *People*, January 20, 1986.

Armstrong, Lisa. "Yasmin Le Bon on the Hardest Thing About Being Married to Simon." *Sydney Morning Herald* (Australia), November 21, 2021.

Heath, Chris. "Mr. and Mrs. Le Bon." *Smash Hits*, January 29–February 11, 1986.

Zaleski, Annie. "30 Years Ago: Duran Duran Strikes Gold Again with 'Come Undone.'" Ultimate Classic Rock, March 29, 2023.

MELISSA ETHERIDGE, "COME TO MY WINDOW" (1993)

Benitez-Eves, Tina. "The Meaning Behind Melissa Etheridge's Pleading Ballad 'Come to My Window.'" *American Songwriter*, 2023.

Etheridge, Melissa with Laurie Morton. *The Truth Is . . .: My Life in Love and Music.* New York: Random House, 2001.

MEAT LOAF, "I'D DO ANYTHING FOR LOVE (BUT I WON'T DO THAT)" (1993)

Meat Loaf. *VH1 Storytellers*, October 18, 1998. https://www.youtube.com/watch?v=5s9RcNO49Cg.

Steinman, Jim. "The Artist's Mind: Jim Steinman on . . ." JimSteinman.com/bat2am.htm.

BOYZ II MEN, "I'LL MAKE LOVE TO YOU" (1994)

Graff, Gary. "Babyface Writes 'Em, Boyz II Men Turns Them into Chart-Smashing Hits." *Ottawa Citizen*, January 5, 1995.

Wertz Jr., Langston. "Love Songs Pay Off for Babyface." *Greenville News* (South Carolina), February 3, 1995.

ELTON JOHN, "CAN YOU FEEL THE LOVE TONIGHT" (1994)

Brevet, Brad. "'X-Men' & 'Alice' Lead Soft Memorial Day Weekend; Disney Tops $4 Billion Worldwide." *Box Office News*, May 29, 2016.

Dibdin, Emma. "The Lyrics and Original Meaning Behind the Lion King's 'Can You Feel the Love Tonight?'" Oprah Daily, June 24, 2019.

Rawden, Jessica. "Why the Lion King Didn't Have Timon and Pumbaa Sing Can You Feel the Love Tonight." CinemaBlend, August 22, 2017.

Troy-Pryde, Jadie. "Apparently 75% of Marriages Fail because of This Wedding Song." *Marie Claire* (UK), September 23, 2020.

CELINE DION, "BECAUSE YOU LOVED ME" (1996)

Evans Price, Debora. "Diane Warren: An Overall Songwriter." *American Songwriter*, 1996.

Hurst, Jack. "The Ballad of Diane Warren." *Chicago Tribune*, August 22, 1999.

K-CI & JOJO, "ALL MY LIFE" (1997)

Kinnon, Joy Bennett. "K-Ci & JoJo: Music's Hottest Duo." *Ebony*, October 1998.

Smith, Shawnee. "K-Ci & JoJo Keep It Clean: Jodeci Singers Go It Alone on MCA." *Billboard*, June 7, 1997.

SAVAGE GARDEN, "TRULY MADLY DEEPLY" (1997)

Caulfield, Keith. "Darren Hayes Talks Savage Garden's 'Truly' Big AC No. 1." *Billboard*, July 15, 2011.

Jones, Carys. "Darren Hayes Savage Garden Interview." Entertainment Focus, February 4, 2016.

SHANIA TWAIN, "YOU'RE STILL THE ONE" (1997)

Morse, Steve. "New Confidence: Singer Shania Twain Builds on Her Free-Spirited Style with a New CD, 'Come on Over.'" *Boston Globe*, November 11, 1997.

LONESTAR, "AMAZED" (1999)

Eames, Tom. "The Story of . . . 'Amazed' by Lonestar." Smooth Radio, June 15, 2023.

"Lonestar's 'Amazed' Voted Most Popular Song for Wedding First Dances." *Telegraph* (UK), July 29, 2009.

Moore, Jayne. "Aimee Mayo Co-Writes #1 Hit 'Amazed' for Lonestar, Plus Other Top Country Hits." SongwriterUniverse. https://www.songwriteruniverse.com/mayo.htm.

O'Flanagan, Corey. *Pitch List* podcast. SongFacts, March 3, 2021.

Tingle, Lauren. "Boyz II Men Uncovers Hidden 'Amazed' History." *CMT*, April 1, 2019.

BRITNEY SPEARS, "SOMETIMES" (1999)
"Interview: JIVE's Steve Lunt." *The Original Doll with James Rodriguez* podcast, February 1, 2023.

NSYNC, "THIS I PROMISE YOU" (2000)
Tailor, Leena. "NSYNC's 'No Strings Attached' Turns 20: How Destiny's Child, Heartache & Lawsuit Fueled the Album (Exclusive)." *Entertainment Tonight*, March 20, 2020.

JOHN MAYER, "YOUR BODY IS A WONDERLAND" (2001)
Interview with John Mayer. *Call Her Daddy* podcast, December 21, 2022. https://www.youtube.com/watch?v=hn8qEhXxuB8.
John Mayer. *VH1 Storytellers*, January 28, 2010. https://www.youtube.com/watch?v=djgxDEpb-Bc.
Snierson, Dan. "Jennifer Love Hewitt Faces Stupid Questions." *Entertainment Weekly*, October 11, 2007.

VANESSA CARLTON, "A THOUSAND MILES" (2002)
Gentile, Dan. "Video of Puppet Singing Vanessa Carlton in San Francisco Goes Viral." SFGATE, May 3, 2023.
Moss, Corey. "Road to the Grammys: The Making of Vanessa Carlton's 'A Thousand Miles.'" MTV News, February 12, 2003.
"The Story of 'A Thousand Miles' by Vanessa Carlton." *Vice*, April 11, 2021. https://www.youtube.com/watch?v=GLO_57IV6Zc.

T.A.T.U., "ALL THE THINGS SHE SAID" (2002)
Girdwood, Barton, and Jessica Placzek. "t.A.T.u's 'All the Things She Said' Still Runs through Our Heads." NPR, September 6, 2022.
Kuipers, Dean. "Techno-Pop t.A.T.u. and Pop-Country (Yes, as in Nashville) Bering Strait Are Making Moves in the US. Is It the Beginning of an Invasion?" *Los Angeles Times*, February 5, 2003.

Snapes, Laura. "Trevor Horn on Grace Jones, Smoking with Malcolm McLaren, and Why Video Didn't Kill the Radio Star." *Guardian*, July 23, 2019.
"t.A.T.u.—Behind the Scenes (Pt. 2)." https://www.youtube.com/watch?v=OclH4d-w8h8.

BEYONCÉ, "CRAZY IN LOVE" (2003)
D'Angelo, Joe. "Road to the Grammys: The Making of Beyonce's 'Crazy in Love.'" MTV News, February 3, 2004.
Garfield, Simon. "Uh-oh! Uh-oh! Uh-oh!" *Guardian*, December 14, 2003.

JOSH GROBAN, "YOU RAISE ME UP" (2003)
Østbø, Stein. "Løvland Is Celebrating that 'You Raise Me Up' Is Ten Years Old." VG, November 13, 2011.

ALICIA KEYS, "IF I AIN'T GOT YOU" (2003)
"Alicia Keys Says Aaliyah Inspired 'If I Ain't Got You': 'The Voice' Story Behind the Song," video. *Billboard*. https://www.billboard.com/video/alicia-keys-says-aaliyah-inspired-if-i-aint-got-you-the-voice-story-behind-the-song-7717160.
Gracie, Bianca. "We've Got a File on You: Alicia Keys." *Stereogum*, September 18, 2020.
Osei, Anthony. "Alicia Keys Says 'If I Ain't Got You' Was Inspired By Aaliyah's Death." *Complex*, June 9, 2011.

YEAH YEAH YEAHS, "MAPS" (2003)
"Karen O's Video Crying Was for Real." WENN, July 12, 2007.
Sheffield, Rob. "Yeah Yeah Yeahs: Goth, Nerd, Slut." *Rolling Stone*, October 7, 2006.
Willman, Chris. "Dr. Luke: The Billboard Cover Story." *Billboard*, September 3, 2010.

DEATH CAB FOR CUTIE, "I WILL FOLLOW YOU INTO THE DARK" (2005)
Clark, Rick. "Death Cab for Cutie: Growing in the Studio, Making Plans." *Mix*, January 1, 2006.

Hanna, Steven. "Death Cab for Cutie: The Plan Hearafter." *Chord*, August–September 2005.

Trendell, Andrew. "Death Cab for Cutie Tell Us About the Meaning and Making of 'I Will Follow You into the Dark.'" *NME*, July 19, 2018.

ADELE, "MAKE YOU FEEL MY LOVE" (2008)

Zaleski, Annie. "'It Speaks Straight from the Heart': Bryan Ferry, Adele and Engelbert Humperdinck on Bob Dylan's Make You Feel My Love." *Guardian*, January 31, 2023.

TAYLOR SWIFT, "LOVE STORY" (2008)

"10 Questions for Taylor Swift." *Time*, April 23, 2009. https://web.archive. org/web/20120531092027/http:// www.time.com/time/magazine/ article/0,9171,1893502,00.html.

Walsh, Christopher. "Taylor Swift—Love Story." *Pro Audio Review*, April 17, 2009. https://web.archive. org/web/20101219201559/http:// proaudioreview.com/article/21158.

USHER, "LOVE IN THIS CLUB" (2008)

Reid, Shaheem. "Usher Chalks Up Song Leaks to 'Internal Conspiracy'—Listen to His New 'Club' Banger Here!" MTV News, February 14, 2008.

Reid, Shaheem. "Young Jeezy Explains How He Got on Usher's 'Love in This Club,' Says Third Album Will Drop 'Sooner Than You Think.'" MTV News, April 30, 2008.

Watson, Margeaux. "Usher: Setting the Record Straight." *Entertainment Weekly*, May 24, 2008.

EDWARD SHARPE AND THE MAGNETIC ZEROS, "HOME" (2009)

Csathy, Peter. "The Story Behind 'Home' and 'Truth,' Edward Sharpe's Companion Songs of Darkness and Light." Consequence of Sound podcast network, March 21, 2022.

Lindner, Emilee. "A Snarky Grandma Is Behind This Emotional Viral TikTok Trend . . . but She Doesn't Exist." *Independent* (UK), February 2, 2021.

McDonald, Scott. "Edward Sharpe, aka Alex Ebert, Finds Himself with the Magnetic Zeros." San Diego News Network, November 6, 2009.

PARAMORE, "THE ONLY EXCEPTION" (2009)

Interview with Hayley Williams. *Alternative Press* and *Kerrang!* https://www. songfacts.com/facts/paramore/the-only-exception.

BRUNO MARS, "JUST THE WAY YOU ARE" (2010)

"ASCAP Grammy Brunch—Bruno Mars Producer Needlz Interview." https://www.youtube.com/ watch?v=KhcmjSbSyPg.

Diehl, Matt. "Bruno Mars' Astronomical Success." *Los Angeles Times*, February 6, 2011.

"Interview with Aaron Bay-Schuck." *HitQuarters*, December 13, 2010.

Lewis, Pete. "Bruno Mars: Out of This World!" *Blues & Soul.* http://www. bluesandsoul.com/feature/593/bruno_ mars_out_of_this_world/.

KATY PERRY, "TEENAGE DREAM" (2010)

Kazemi, Alex. "Single Review of Teenage Dream–Katy Perry / Interview with Its Songwriter Bonnie McKee." AlexKazemi.com. https://web.archive. org/web/20100807001855/http:// alexkazemi.com/2010/07/listensingle-review-teenage-dream-katy-perry/.

RIHANNA, "WE FOUND LOVE" (2011)

"Calvin Harris Explains Why He Ditched Leona Lewis for Rihanna on Number One Hit 'We Found Love.'" *NME*, April 22, 2015.

Vena, Jocelyn. "Rihanna's 'We Found Love' Video Tells 'Everybody's' Story." MTV News, October 21, 2011.

SARA BAREILLES, "I CHOOSE YOU" (2013)

Azzopardi, Chris. "Q&A: Sara Bareilles Talks Gay 'Brothers and Sisters,' Whether Closeted Celebs Are 'Brave' & Why She Thinks Taylor Swift Stands For 'Sisterhood.'" Pride Source, October 8, 2015.

Malec, Brett. "Sara Bareilles Helps Couples Propose in Heartwarming 'I Choose You' Music Video—Watch!" E! Online, May 8, 2014.

JOHN LEGEND, "ALL OF ME" (2013)

Sandell, Laurie. "Chrissy Teigen Is a Member of the Mile-High Club." *Cosmopolitan*, April 28, 2014.

TONY BENNETT AND LADY GAGA, "CHEEK TO CHEEK" (2014)

"Astaire, Rogers Score Again in 'Top Hat' Dance." *Tyler Courier-Times* (Texas), September 8, 1935.

Vivinetto, Gina. "Lady Gaga Shares Tribute to Tony Bennett on What Would Have Been His 97th Birthday." *Today*, August 3, 2023.

"Your Hit Parade Charts 1935–1940." https://archive.org/details/YourHitParadeCharts19351940/page/n13/mode/2up.

ED SHEERAN FEATURING BEYONCÉ, "PERFECT DUET" (2017)

Roth, Madeline. "Hear the Ballad Ed Sheeran Calls 'the Best Love Song' of His Career." MTV News, March 3, 2017.

HARRY STYLES, "ADORE YOU" (2019)

Alston, Trey. "Harry Styles Spilled the Deets on Some Fine Line Songs in New Tiny Desk Concert." MTV News, March 16, 2020.

Burton, Jamie. "Harry Styles Confirms NSFW Meaning Behind 'Watermelon Sugar' Lyrics." *Newsweek*, October 5, 2021.

Sheffield, Rob. "Harry Styles Reveals the Secrets Behind 'Fine Line.'" *Rolling Stone*, December 13, 2019.

Index

About the Author

ANNIE ZALESKI is an author, editor, and journalist with a focus on music and pop culture. Her work has appeared in dozens of publications, including NPR Music, *The Guardian*, *Time*, *Rolling Stone*, *Salon*, *Billboard*, the A.V. Club, *Vulture*, *Alternative Press*, *Stereogum*, *Classic Pop*, the *Los Angeles Times*, and the *Cleveland Plain Dealer*. She is the author of *This Is Christmas, Song by Song*; a book on Duran Duran's *Rio* for the 33⅓ book series; and the illustrated biographies *Lady Gaga: Applause* and *Pink: Raise Your Glass*. She has also contributed essays to the books *Women Who Rock* and *Go All the Way: A Literary Appreciation of Power Pop*. She lives in Cleveland, Ohio.

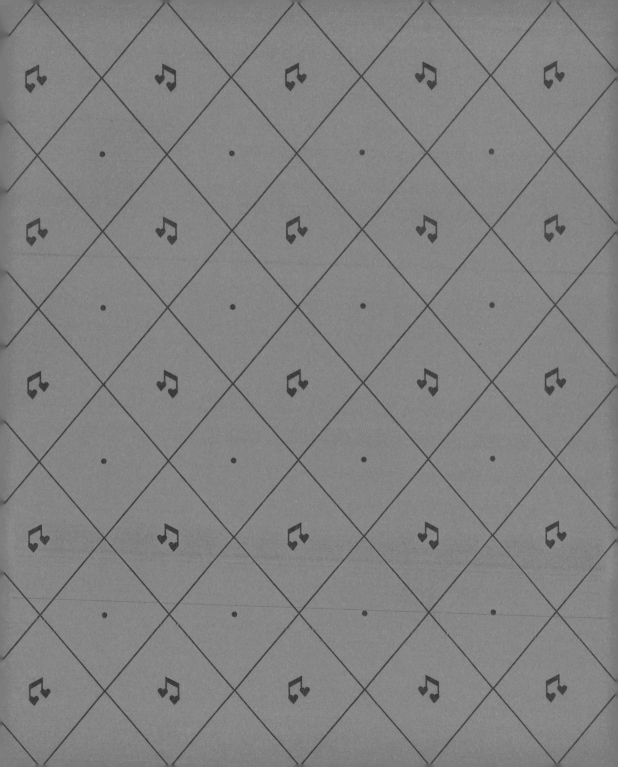

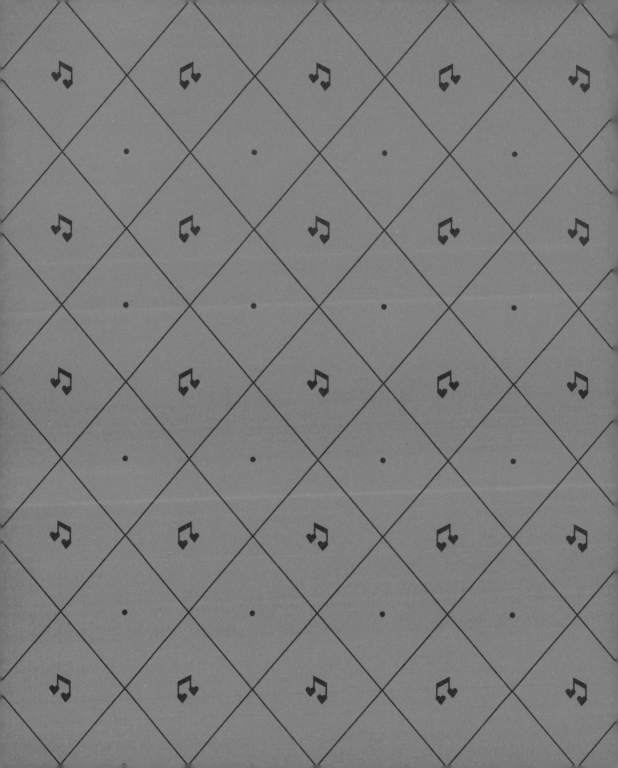